15

The Willie Mays Story

After only two years of playing in organized baseball, Willie Mays came to the New York Giants a frightened young rookie. The rest is baseball history. Willie led the Giants to a miracle stretch drive that won the 1951 pennant and earned him the Rookie of the Year award. Then, after two years in the Army, he led the Giants to a world's championship and won the National League's Most Valuable Player award. Willie is still the team's veteran pillar of strength and the highest paid Giant player in history.

Books by Milton J. Shapiro

The Sal Maglie Story

Jackie Robinson of the Brooklyn Dodgers

The Warren Spahn Story

The Roy Campanella Story

The Phil Rizzuto Story

The Mel Ott Story

The Willie Mays Story

The Gil Hodges Story

The Hank Aaron Story

A Beginner's Book of Sporting Guns
and Hunting

Mickey Mantle: Yankee Slugger

The Whitey Ford Story

The Dizzy Dean Story

WILLIE MAYS,
DUKE SNIDER
AND DON MUELLER
AT EBBETS FIELD
(1953)

FOUR GIANTS WHO HIT
HOME RUNS IN DEFEATING
THE DODGERS—
AL DARK, MONTE IRVIN,
WES WESTRUM, WILLIE MAYS
(1953)

WILLIE ELUDES TAG
BY DODGER PITCHER
JOHNNY PODRES
(1957)

WILLIE MAYS AND HIS
MANAGER LEO DUROCHER
IN SPRING TRAINING
(1955)

WILLIE MAYS AND
GIANTS' MANAGER
BILL RIGNEY
(1959)

YOGI BERRA AND WILLIE MAYS HO
THEIR MOST VALUABLE PLAYER PLAQUI
WHILE JOHNNY ANTONELLI WAS VOT
THE GIANTS' ACE PITCHER (1955)

WILLIE MAYS CATCHING LONG DRIVE BY
VIC WERTZ IN 1954 WORLD SERIES

WILLIE MAYS, HIS WIFE MARGHU-
RITE AND BABY SON MICHAEL
(1959)

THE
WILLIE MAYS
STORY

by Milton J. Shapiro

Julian Messner   New York

Published by Julian Messner, Inc.
8 West 40 Street, New York 18

Published simultaneously in Canada
by The Copp Clark Publishing Co. Limited

© Copyright 1960 by Milton J. Shapiro

Sixth Printing, 1964

Photographs used with the permission of
Wide World Photos

Printed in the United States of America
Library of Congress Catalog Card No. 60–7055

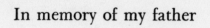
In memory of my father

With grateful acknowledgment to
Bill Carr for his help
in the preparation
of this book

THE TOWN OF FAIRFIELD, ALABAMA, LAY OVEN HOT UNDER the July sun. Walking briskly down Merriam Street, a spring in his step despite the heat and the gray at his temples, Walter Mays turned in at number 28, and began to whistle cheerfully as he climbed the stairs in the musty hallway. He always felt good when it came time to visit his grandson Willie. At the second floor landing he stopped and put his ear to the door, smiled, rapped lightly and walked in without waiting for an answer.

"Hey, where's my boy Willie!" he called, poking his head around the edge of the door.

From the kitchen to his right toddled a little boy, clad only in a diaper against the oppressive heat. He waddled a few steps, fell, picked himself up, and teetered forward again, arms outstretched. His grandfather squatted to meet him and lifted him in his arms. "Look at that boy walk!" he exulted, eyes sparkling. He looked up as the youngster's mother entered the room, drying her hands on an apron. "Ann, did you see how that boy Willie walked!" he exclaimed.

She smiled. "Why not? He's fourteen months old," she teased. "Time he was walking, isn't it?"

11

Walter Mays rose to the bait. "Yeah? Well you should have seen that husband of yours at this age, crawling all over the place, lazy as you please. Didn't walk till he was a year and a half, more maybe."

Ann Mays laughed. "Well, Grandpa Mays, he was *your* son."

He grinned at her, suddenly realizing she was teasing him. "Where is William, by the way?"

"Today's Saturday, remember? He's down at that field by the railroad yards, playing baseball."

"Oh, say, that reminds me," Walter Mays said. He put Willie down on the floor, reached into his pocket and withdrew a white rubber ball. "Look what I got for you, Willie," he addressed the youngster. He moved to the far end of the room, stooped, rolled the ball across the floor. Willie scampered toward it on all fours, reached out a hand and clutched it neatly. Then unsteadily he rose to his feet and, with a little wave of his right arm, threw it back toward his grandfather.

"Hey! Just like Tris Speaker!" chuckled Walter Mays. "Yessir, Annie, this boy of yours is a Mays all right. Gonna play ball just like his father and his grandpop here."

"Better than that, I hope," she laughed, "or he'd be smarter spending his Saturdays down at the mill."

He held up his hands in mock horror. "Oh, say, Annie, we don't want no tin mill for this boy. No, sir. We want something better than that for little Willie here. Don't we, Willie?" He squatted in front of his grandson and tousled his hair.

Willie gurgled, toddled off after the ball again. He bent, picked it up, turned and threw it across the room.

"Look at that wing," Walter Mays marveled. "Yeah, just like Tris Speaker." His eyes went dreamy for a moment. "No, no tin mill for you, Willie boy." he said softly. "Maybe —" he set his lips and laughed shortly. "Walter Mays, you're

12

thinking like an old fool," he said half to himself. He stood up then and turned to leave. "Guess I'll wander down to the yards and watch the game," he said. "See you tomorrow maybe, Ann. So long, Willie," he waved. But Willie was absorbed in play, chasing the white rubber ball around the room.

Whatever lofty dreams Walter Mays might have held for his grandson that summer of 1932, they hardly seemed likely to come true. Walter Mays had been a semiprofessional pitcher; his son, William Howard Mays, made an extra dollar on an occasional weekend playing the outfield on a semipro team; but at best baseball was an avocation for a Negro. Even the professional Negro League paid hardly more than a good job in a factory.

As for Willie himself, barely a year old, if he dreamed at all it was of sterner stuff. Reality was as close as his open bedroom window, where the sill lay covered with the soot that unendingly drifted in from the smoking chimneys of the nearby tin and steel mills, where on summer nights he could hear the chug-chug of the freight engines in the switching yards close by, and see the red glow of open hearth fires against the night sky.

When Willie was two years old his parents were divorced. His mother married a man named Frank McMorris and Willie went to live with his Aunt Sarah, his mother's sister. Willie's father moved to a room just a few blocks away, and both his mother and father came regularly to Aunt Sarah's to see him.

Willie could run almost as soon as he could walk, and before long the streets of Fairfield rang with the happy shrieks of the youngster and his friends. If it was a game that required speed afoot, like tag or ring-o-leevio, Willie couldn't be caught, and by the time he was in fourth grade at elementary school he was fast enough and strong enough to play baseball with boys many years older.

As is often the case in sandlot baseball, the standout player was chosen to pitch, and so Willie pitched. He didn't know how to throw a curve, but he threw fast and straight, and often on weekends his father and grandfather would stand on the sidelines and cheer him on. Until one Sunday the gleam in Walter Mays's eyes faded, and the smile on his lips became a frown as he watched Willie toiling on the mound.

After the game he walked home with his grandson, his arm draped around the boy's shoulders. "Willie," he said, "you gotta cut out this pitching business."

Willie turned, his eyes startled. "Cut out pitching? What are you talking about, Grandpa? I thought you and Pop wanted me to play baseball?" Suddenly an idea flicked at his mind and he pouted. "Aw, I'll bet Aunt Sarah's been getting on you because sometimes I miss Sunday school on account of a game. It only—"

"No, no, nothing like that," Walter Mays soothed him. "And don't you be getting sore at your Aunt Sarah, Willie. You know she's on your side one hundred per cent, and if she gets after you for something it's because she wants you to grow up good, that's all. But this pitching, it's got nothing to do with all that. I'm just afraid you're gonna kill your arm before you even get really started playing baseball."

"Kill my arm!" Willie protested. "You saw me play today, Grandpa. Struck out six guys, and I was still able to hit a home run in the eighth inning!"

"Yeah, but I saw the way you were breathing mighty hard, too, the last couple of innings, and you like to near fell down running out that homer. I'm telling you, Willie, look at what happened to me. Pitched too much sandlot baseball when I was a kid, using them soft, cheap baseballs like you're doing, and by the time I got to play semipro I was near pitched out.

14

Couple of good years, then the hop on my fast one was gone. And 'fore I knew it, I was gone."

Willie nodded soberly. "Gee, I guess I never thought of it that way, Grandpa."

"Wouldn't expect a ten-year-old to think about what's gonna be when he's twenty," his grandfather said. "Wouldn't be natural, I guess. But you're a sensible boy, Willie. You listen to older folks who know better than you, I've noticed that. And it's gonna do you a lot of good later on. So now you listen to your grandpa and leave the pitching to some other kids. You grab your glove and take it to the outfield."

They walked along quietly for a while, then, when they reached Willie's house, Walter Mays spoke again. "You know, Willie, Jim McWilliams has been talking to me about you."

"Jim McWilliams?" Willie scratched his head. "Who's Jim McWilliams?"

"Jim's coach at Fairfield Industrial High School," his grandfather explained. "I know Jim from the years I was playing semipro ball. Anyway, seems a couple of the guys you've been striking out regularly play basketball and football for Fairfield, and lately they've been telling McWilliams about how good you are."

Willie kicked lamely at a nonexistent pebble. "Aw, I'm not that all good."

His grandfather chuckled. "Maybe not, but from talking to McWilliams I got the idea he can't wait to get his clutches on you."

"What for? Fairfield doesn't even have a baseball team."

"No, but they got football and basketball teams. You play football and basketball, don't you?"

"Sure, but—"

"Well, McWilliams will see to it that you play them at Fairfield, too," Walter Mays said. "You're a natural-born athlete, Willie. McWilliams can tell just from hearing about you."

15

"Gee, it's a shame though they don't have a baseball team," Willie said. "I was kind of hoping I could go to a high school that had a baseball team," he added hesitantly.

Walter Mays sighed. "Those things aren't for me to say, Willie. That's for your mother and father and your Aunt Sarah to tell you. But you know the boys around here all go to Fairfield, and that's probably where you'll go, so you might as well figure on it. Besides, you can learn a good trade there."

"But I don't really want to learn a trade, Grandpa. I want to play baseball—and how am I going to play if Fairfield doesn't even have a team?"

"You just leave that to me and your pa. We'll be working right with you, Willie, teaching you all we know. Your pa is gonna start taking you to his games and showing you the ropes—I'll talk to him about that—and you play all the ball you can on the pickup teams around here. But remember— in the outfield, Willie."

Willie nodded. "I'll remember, Grandpa."

"Good. And later on, when you're ready to get out of high school—well, time enough then to worry about what's gonna be." Walter Mays patted his grandson's head affectionately and turned to leave.

"That you, Willie?" Aunt Sarah's voice came from inside the house.

"Yes, Aunt Sarah," Willie called back. "I'm out here with Grandpa."

Aunt Sarah poked her head out the window. "There you go again, Grandpa Mays, keeping Willie out playing baseball when he should be home doing his schoolwork." But she smiled as she scolded, and Walter Mays grinned back at her.

"You're worse than an old mother hen, Aunt Sarah. A boy's got to play, too. And Willie here, he's playing for something important someday."

16

"Well, today eating's important, and Willie's supper is getting cold. Why don't you come inside and join us, Grandpa Mays? Got roast ham and sweet potatoes."

But he waved at her with a smile. "No, thank you just the same, Aunt Sarah. I'm gonna wander off and walk awhile. You go ahead inside, Willie," he said to his grandson. He waited until the youngster entered the house, then spoke to Aunt Sarah.

"Treat that boy kindly, Aunt Sarah," he said quietly. "He's a good boy. And someday he's gonna be somebody big. I just feel it in my soul."

2

THE QUARTERBACK IN THE GOLD AND CRIMSON OF FAIRFIELD lifted his head from the huddle and squinted at the clock on the scoreboard. Only seven minutes left to play and Fairfield was on its own twenty-six-yard line, trailing Birmingham High, 19–7. He bent into the huddle again and spoke swiftly. "Okay, guys, number sixty-six to the left, on three, and let's give Willie some running room this time. Let's go!"

The huddle broke open. The linemen knelt in position and the backfield shifted into a T formation. The quarterback crouched behind the center, began to call the signals.

"Forty-one . . . thirty-seven . . . eleven . . ." A swift surge of motion as the ball was snapped back. The linemen charged; the Fairfield quarterback swiveled, faked a hand-off to a plunging fullback to his right, then pitched the ball underhand across his body to the halfback who was loafing toward the right sideline. The halfback—Willie Mays—grabbed the pitchout and shifted into full speed, hitting the line of scrimmage like a juggernaut. He barreled into and over the Birmingham left end, side-stepped the linebacker, picked up his own running guard for interference and raced up field.

18

He reached the thirty-five-yard line, the forty, at the forty-five his guard cut down a defenseman and now he was alone. He tore past the midfield stripe, the roar of the crowd acting like a spur; then through the roar came the sound of desperate pursuit on the frozen turf. Down past the Birmingham forty-yard line he ran, and out of the corner of his eye spied the two enemy players straining to cut him off. Calculating as he ran, Willie suddenly shifted his gears, slowed down quickly, swiveled his hips and circled around to his left. The Birmingham players, caught off stride, couldn't change their pace in time. They overran Willie, waving at him futilely as he reversed his field around them, picked up speed again—and was free. The goal posts loomed before him. He ran joyously down field, to the twenty-five . . . the twenty . . . the ten—and Willie was over for the touchdown!

The drums pounded and the stands rang with cheers. "Yee-ay, Mays! Yee-ay, Mays! Yee-ay, Mays! TEAM TEAM TEAM!"

The officials placed the ball on the two-yard line and the team lined up for the extra point try. The ball was snapped back, the Fairfield fullback kicked it into the air—good! Between the goal posts for the extra point.

The score now was Birmingham nineteen, Fairfield fourteen. Less than six minutes remained to play and Fairfield, as scorers, had to kick off to Birmingham. The teams took their positions, the whistle blew and Fairfield kicked. Birmingham returned the ball to its own twenty-five and went into a huddle. "We gotta try to keep the ball and kill the clock," the Birmingham quaterback said. "So let's go, men, open up those holes. Forty-two, on four."

On the first play the Birmingham fullback plunged off tackle for four yards. Then it was the quarterback after a fake hand-off for three inside guard. The fullback hit again for four and it was a first down, Birmingham. The left halfback circled end for five yards, the fullback made two, and it was third down and three yards to go for another first down on the Birmingham forty-three. Less than four minutes left to play. Willie Mays, acting as left linebacker on defense, roamed behind the line, exhorting his teammates. "Hold 'em!" he pleaded. "Let's get that ball. One more time! One more time! Hold 'em in there!"

Birmingham tried a double reverse with the halfback circling the Fairfield end. He reached the line of scrimmage and went down hard as Willie Mays came in fast to stop him. Fourth down now and still three yards to go. The Birmingham quarterback looked up at the clock. Three minutes to play. A good punt now would put Fairfield deep in its own territory, he thought. They'd have no choice but to try long passes, and we'd be prepared for that.

He punted on the next play, high and far. Willie Mays picked it out of the air on his own eighteen-yard line and charged up field. He reached the twenty-five, was hit by two men on the thirty but kept going. Hit again on the thirty-three, he staggered, twisted away, charged knees high, head down, was hit on the thirty-five, swarmed over and brought down by a horde of Birmingham players. He rose to his feet, shaky, his head buzzing, and wandered vaguely into the huddle.

"They'll be expecting the long passes, but we got to try it just the same," the Fairfield quarterback said grimly. "Willie, how's your arm?" Willie nodded dazedly, not really comprehending what was asked. He was practically out on his feet.

Fairfield came out of the huddle and lined up. "Eighty-one, forty-six—" the quarterback turned and passed off to Willie, who drifted back to throw a long pass. But the Birmingham linemen charged through, rushing him, grabbing at him. Willie batted one player away with a stiff arm, side-stepped another, but they were closing in on him, there was no chance to pass. Willie searched desperately for a receiver, found none, tucked the ball under his arm and ran.

He got back to the line of scrimmage. A Birmingham player grabbed at him, caught him. Willie twisted away, leaving part of his jersey in the boy's hand. He reached the forty-yard line, was hit once, twice. He fought his way out, feet churning the earth, shoulders and head battering forward, strewing enemy players in his wake. His eyes were glazed as he ran now; he ran, he stumbled, he fought his way up field on instinct, his mind clouded by the pounding he had taken in the last minutes.

The roar of the crowd sounded like a tinny echo. He didn't know how far he had gone. He just kept running . . . running . . . had to run, had to keep going, the clock was running out . . . nobody to pass to . . . had to keep going . . . hands on him, grabbing at him, bodies hitting him . . .

Suddenly he was on the ground. Somebody was on top of him. He fought to get up. Then his head exploded with sound, a roaring in his ears. It was the crowd, cheering, he could hear them clearly, they weren't far away any more. He opened his eyes wide and saw clearly. Saw his own teammate sitting astride his chest, grinning widely. "Hey, man, you like to near run out of the stadium until I pulled you down and sat on you. You scored your touchdown, Willie. Were you figuring on heading right home before the game was over?"

They helped Willie up then and led him off the field, the cheers and the drums chanting their praises for his magnificent display of courage and skill. The score now was Fairfield twenty, Birmingham nineteen, and no one cared that the extra point was missed when the final gun went off a few minutes later.

Willie Mays, fifteen years old and a sophomore, led Fairfield to victory after victory. For a football player he was slightly built, almost skinny, but his speed, his agility, his ability to think under pressure and his accurate passing arm more than made up for his lack of bulk. He brought Fairfield the Jefferson County championship in 1946, scoring twelve touchdowns himself and passing for five more.

When the football season ended Willie continued on to basketball. Playing forward for Fairfield he brought them another county championship and himself the high scorer title for the county. Only during the spring and summer months was he idle in school sports, and then his father and grandfather took over his training in baseball. When he was sixteen Willie joined his father's semipro team and quickly won a reputation in the Fairfield-Birmingham area as a deadly hitter and superb outfielder.

In the spring of 1948 Grandfather Mays came to Aunt Sarah's house and said it was time to plan his grandson's future. "Willie will be graduating from school in June," he said. "We ought to decide what's gonna be with the boy."

"He did good in school," Aunt Sarah said. "He can get a good job anyplace."

Walter Mays turned to his grandson. "How about it, Willie?"

Willie shifted nervously. "Well, Grandpa, I graduate as a certified laundry presser, but I sure don't want to go to work in a laundry."

"How about the mills?" his father suggested. "I can get you in where I work. Or any of the steel mills around will be glad to get you. You picked up some muscle the past couple of years."

"No!" Walter Mays thundered. "Willie, I warn you, don't go near the mills. Not one day! Once you start working in a mill you're finished. You'll never get out. Look at what happened to me and your father."

"Nothing wrong with you," Willie said sullenly.

"Not much right, either," his grandfather countered. "But at least we had an excuse. There wasn't much else for us to do, except work in one kind of mill or another. You can do better."

"What are you aiming at, Grandfather Mays?" Aunt Sarah said. "You got something on your mind. I know you. C'mon, out with it."

Walter Mays looked around the room slowly, savoring the moment. "You all read in the papers about Jackie Robinson playing with the Brooklyn Dodgers?"

"Sure, everybody has," said Willie's father. "He's done a great thing."

Walter Mays sat back in his chair. "Well?" he said smugly.

Aunt Sarah looked at him narrowly. "You mean Willie—?"

"Why not?" Walter Mays said.

"Yeah, why not?" Willie's father said excitedly. "Willie's a great baseball player, everybody 'round here knows that. Why couldn't he make the major leagues like Jackie Robinson?"

"Cause it's plain foolishness, that's why," snapped Aunt Sarah. "Why are you two crazy lunatics gettin' up a boy's hopes with your wild dreaming when you know darn well Willie's got one chance in a million of playing in the major leagues?"

"It ain't one in a million!" Walter Mays countered. "Not any more it ain't. Can't you see what happened, Aunt Sarah? A colored boy's got a good chance now, with Robinson makin' it, and men like Roy Campanella and Don Newcombe in the minor leagues, ready to come up any day. Maybe it ain't as good a chance as if he was white—not yet— but it's an honest to goodness chance. And Willie here is gonna get his, if I got anything to say about it!"

"How about somebody asking me?" Willie said suddenly.

The three adults looked at him; they had forgotten his presence in the heat of their discussion. "Well, how about it, Willie?" his father asked quietly.

"Well, while you three have been arguing, I've been thinking. Fact is, I've been thinking for a couple of years. I'll tell you this, Aunt Sarah. You brought me up good, like you was

23

my own mother, and I respect what you think. I know you want what's right for me, and . . . and, well, you're a practical woman, Aunt Sarah. But I don't want to work in any steel mill or tin mill or laundry. Grandpa's right. Once I went into a mill I'd never get out."

Aunt Sarah looked down at the hands folded in her lap. "What do you want, then, Willie?"

"To play baseball. More than anything else in the world, I want to play baseball."

Aunt Sarah sighed. "And you, Grandfather Mays, and you, William Mays, you think this is possible for a boy like Willie? To play baseball for a living?"

"Sure it is!" Walter Mays said. His son nodded agreement.

She sighed. "Well then, what do we do next?"

Willie clapped his hands in delight. "Atta girl, Aunt Sarah!"

Walter Mays grinned. "I got it all figured out. William," he said to Willie's father, "we got to get this boy some professional experience, and someplace where he's gonna make the folks sit up and take notice."

"Like where?" William Mays asked.

"This Saturday you and me are taking Willie to see Piper Davis."

"And who's this Piper Davis?" Aunt Sarah asked.

"Manager of the Birmingham Barons," Walter Mays explained. "The Negro League."

"You think they'll take me on?" Willie asked anxiously.

His father nodded. "I'll bet he will. He's been around our games plenty of times, watching us play. He knows what you can do."

"Are you men forgetting Willie still has to finish school?" Aunt Sarah said.

"I'm not forgetting," Walter Mays said. "Until Willie graduates he can play only the weekends when the Barons are home."

24

"Yeah, that's right, Grandpa," Willie said. "And soon as school is over I can start playing full time, traveling with them and everything."

Walter Mays nodded. "The major league scouts have their eyes on the Negro League these days. And after what Willie can show 'em, he'll be grabbed up in no time, mark my words."

"And if he isn't?" said Aunt Sarah.

"But I will be!" Willie said defiantly. "I will be, Aunt Sarah! Why do you always have to think about the bad side of things!"

Aunt Sarah bit her lip. "Willie, I don't call it lookin' at the bad side of things just because I look at all the sides. I've seen too much disappointment, too many high hopes fall flat on their faces to believe that everything comes out all right in the end. It don't, Willie, and I believe in being prepared for the fall as well as for the climbing. That way you don't get hurt so much if it turns out that you do fall."

"Willie won't fall," his father said. "He's too good, Aunt Sarah. I can tell you that with all the faith I got in the world."

"And if he should fall, by some bad luck," Walter Mays added, "he's got all of us here to catch him. The steel mills, the good Lord forbid, will always he here, too."

"Amen," said Aunt Sarah solemnly.

3

DAN INGRAM, PITCHER FOR THE KANSAS CITY MONARCHS OF the Negro League, stood on the mound and appraised the youngster dug in at home plate, swinging his bat menacingly. The kid couldn't be more than seventeen or so, Ingram thought. Stands up there like a veteran, though. Willie Mays was his name. Old Walt Mays's grandson. Ingram, a veteran of many years in the Negro League, had heard vaguely of Walter Mays's pitching prowess among the semipros in the Birmingham area. Ingram was tempted for a moment to give Walter Mays's grandson a break. But no, that wasn't the way.

Ingram swung into a windup and threw a curve that broke inside sharply. Willie hung in close to the plate, waited until the last possible moment, then leaned back quickly to avoid being hit. "Ball one!" the umpire called. On the mound Dan Ingram smiled. Not afraid of the close ones, eh? Well, Willie boy, let's see how you like a high hard one right over the plate. He wound up, came down with a blazing fast ball. Willie set himself, swung, cracked the pitch on a long line to left center field. It bounced between the outfielders and rolled to the wall. Willie already was rounding first. He dug for second, didn't stop, sped for third. His cap blew off as

26

he charged down the base paths. He stopped short, retrieved his cap, resumed his race for third base. The throw came in, Willie slid headlong. The umpire peered through the cloud of dust. "Safe!" he bawled, spreading his hands palms down. Willie Mays had the first base hit of his professional Negro League career.

But manager Piper Davis was less than impressed. He was nearly livid with rage and incredulity. A moment later, when Willie scored on a single, Davis cornered him in the dugout. "You crazy or something, Willie? Or maybe you're one of those showboat boys?"

Willie looked at him blankly. "What do you mean, Mr. Davis? I do something wrong?"

"Wrong! You want to know if you did something wrong?" He peered closely at Willie's face, trying to determine whether Willie was actually as guileless as he looked or merely a good actor. "How come you stopped in the middle of running out a triple to pick up your cap?"

Willie's face remained expressionless. " 'Cause it came off," he said. "I didn't think much about it. I just stopped, I guess."

"Yeah, and what if you got tagged out at third because you stopped for that fool cap?" Davis still couldn't believe that Willie wasn't up to some scheme or clownishness.

"Oh, I had one eye on the relay all the time, Mr. Davis," Willie explained eagerly, anxious to appease his manager. "I knew I still had time to make third okay."

Davis' jaw opened, then closed silently. He stared unbelievingly at this brash, yet ingenuous youngster who calculated so coolly in his first game of professional baseball. Sent up to pinch-hit and acts as though he had been hitting triples all his life. "Well, next time run out your hit first, then go back for your cap," was the Barons' pilot lame reply.

"Yessir, I'll do that, Mr. Davis," Willie said.

But Willie did not always keep the promise. Not through

stubbornness, or carelessness, or deliberate design. It was just that Willie Mays's cap had a way of flying off as he flashed around the base paths, and likely as not Willie would stop and retrieve it before going on, depending on whether or not he thought he had time. It happened at times while Willie was patrolling the outfield, too. Playing in the Kansas City park one day, Willie began chasing a fly ball to deep center field. As he ran his cap blew off. He stopped, picked it up, put it on, then resumed his chase. At the last moment he reached out, his back to home plate, and plucked the ball right off the wall.

The fans roared at his spectacular catch—and it was spectacular, under the circumstances—but again manager Piper Davis was threatened with apoplexy. "Willie, you'll give me a stroke before you're done," he said wearily in the dugout later. Yet Davis had to admit that Willie was indeed a wonder. He had started the youngster as a utility outfielder and pinch hitter, but when Willie had graduated from school in June, and coincidentally the Barons' center fielder had been injured, Davis had crossed his fingers and installed him in center field. That was a month ago, and considering that Willie's fielding sparkled and he was hitting better than .300, Davis was hardly likely to bench him. But had he tried it anyway, the Birmingham fans would have torn down the park in protest and run him out of town. For in the short period of one month young Willie Mays had become one of the most popular players in the Barons' history.

"What a treat to watch this young fly hawk play ball," a reporter for the Birmingham newspaper wrote about Willie. "He seems to lope over the outfield like a happy gazelle, or like a retriever dog sent to bring back a stick. You get the impression young Willie Mays's happiest moments are those spent in pursuit of a baseball."

Willie returned from the Barons' first road trip laden with presents and tales of wonder about the places he had been.

28

On the Barons' schedule were such clubs as the New York Cubans, the Cincinnati Clowns, the Kansas City Monarchs and Pittsburgh's Homestead Grays. He was especially impressed with the immenseness of the Polo Grounds, where he played against the Cubans. "Pop, you've never seen such an outfield in your life," he said to his father. "You can run nine miles and still have room to catch a ball out there. It's nearly five hundred feet straightaway in center field!"

"That's a good outfield for a boy like you," his father commented. "With plenty of running room they ain't gonna hit many past you, Willie."

"Well, they haven't so far, anyway," Willie said modestly. "Say Aunt Sarah," he turned to his aunt, "you like those earrings and things I brought you from New York?"

"They're beautiful, Willie, but you shouldn't be going around spending your money like that. It's more than enough that you send me and your pa money every month."

"Heck, Aunt Sarah, what for do I need money? I got a dollar in my pocket and a lot of friends and I'm playing baseball every day. What else is there?"

Willie's generosity extended to his mother and stepfather, too. They had ten children now, and Willie went around to the house and left them money, and later, when he returned to the road, he saw to it that money was mailed to them every month.

Willie batted .312 that first season with the Birmingham Barons, and when he returned for spring training in 1949 he was considered an established star though not quite eighteen years old. Despite the respect for his baseball talents, however, his teammates treated him like a maverick kid brother. Most of the Barons were veterans who had knocked about the Negro League for many years. Since Jackie Robinson broke the color line in organized baseball in 1946, they had seen the top men in their league go on to follow in Robinson's trail-blazing footsteps. The Barons had played against men like Roy Campanella, Don Newcombe, Dan Bankhead, Monte Irvin, Sam Jethroe, Luke Easter and Larry Doby, all of whom had made the major leagues. The players who remained behind in the Negro League felt that the opportunity to rise into major league baseball had passed them by, that only the youngsters like Willie Mays had a chance now. But instead of bitterness or jealousy, they demonstrated a willingness to help boost Willie along. They teased him and kidded him and made him the butt of their practical jokes. But they taught him much, too.

Willie began his second season with the Barons determined to prove that his rookie year was no fluke. He ran with joyous abandon in the outfield and on the base paths. He raked pitchers on every team in the league, right-handers or left, it made no difference to Willie. When he read in a newspaper story that all he needed was a little more base stealing skill to become a truly dangerous runner, he set out to prove the reporter had underrated him. The next day, playing against the Kansas City Monarchs, he singled his first time up and stole second on the first pitch. On the next pitch he took off for third, but the Monarch catcher, alert now, rifled a throw to the third baseman. The ball, Willie, and the third baseman disappeared in a cloud of dust as Willie dived headfirst for the base. A split second later the ball came trickling away into foul ground. In his slide, Willie had knocked the ball out of the third baseman's hands. He got up, grinning, as the Birmingham crowd cheered his thievery.

The Monarchs' third baseman rose slowly, sheepishly. "Hey, Willie," Hank Thompson said, "you ain't on the football field now. You hit me like that again I'm gonna put in a request for hip pads."

Willie chuckled and nudged Thompson with his elbow. "I always asked the boss if I could wear my old football helmet, but he says it's illegal. Now how about that?"

By midseason Willie was belting the ball at a .350 pace and

leading the Barons in runs batted in. It was a foregone conclusion to everybody on the team that the major league scouts would camp on Willie's tail any day, and in August of 1949 they came. A Dodger scout appeared first. He sat in the Birmingham ball park for several days, sent there on the advice of Jackie Robinson who had heard about Mays from friends in the Negro League. The report went back to Brooklyn: "Mays won't do. He's weak on curve balls."

The Yankees sent a man out. He watched Mays in the Polo Grounds, against the New York Cubans. In a three-game series there Willie hit a triple, two doubles and two singles in fourteen times at bat. But the scout reported back to the Yankees that he was unsure in his fielding and needed a few more years' experience.

Willie never knew these scouts were trailing him. His teammates knew. Manager Piper Davis knew. But they didn't want their eighteen-year-old star to feel the pressure of playing before big league scouts. If they wanted him, fine, he'd learn about it soon enough. If they turned him down—as two had done so far—he wouldn't feel the disappointment.

In September of 1949 the Braves sent a scout out who liked Willie well enough to recommend his purchase, although he had reservations because of Willie's inexperience. When the Braves made their offer to the Barons' owners they stipulated that if Mays failed to make the grade in the majors their purchase price would be refunded. The Barons refused this kind of deal, so when the 1949 season ended and Willie had batted a fine .311, he still seemed years away from the major leagues.

After the season Willie joined the Barons in a barnstorming tour around the country in which they played exhibitions against an All-Star team of Negro major leaguers. Willie had been reluctant to go along on the tour, for though he loved to play baseball, at that time he preferred to remain home with his family. But manager Davis told him of the tour's

31

importance. "It ain't the extra couple of bucks you'll make that counts," he said. "But you'll be playing against some of the top boys in the major leagues, hitting against Newcombe, Satchel Paige, Dan Bankhead. Jackie Robinson will be there, and Roy Campanella. These guys carry weight. They like what they see in you and they'll report it back to their bosses."

Willie agreed to the tour. It was to last two months and cover twenty-three major cities throughout the country. In his first three games against the All-Stars Willie was unimpressive. Manager Davis, who was sincerely trying to get him a major league contract, chafed at Willie's poor hitting and indifferent fielding. "Maybe just having a bad streak," he said to himself, for Willie was a streak hitter. But Davis couldn't quite believe it. At the end of a week, during which Willie had not only failed to get one extra-base hit, but let fall safely fly balls he ordinarily would have caught with ease, Davis was at his wits' end. He was about to bench Willie when a teammate solved the puzzle.

"Hey," he said to the Barons' manager one morning. "You know Willie's homesick?"

"Homesick?" Davis repeated incredulously.

"Yeah. I found out last night. I wanted him to go to the movies with me, and you know Willie, he'll see the same picture three times—he don't care so long as he's sitting in a movie. But he didn't want to go. He just sat there in his room reading a letter. 'What you got there, Willie?' I asked him. 'Letter from my Aunt Sarah,' he said. He didn't even look up at me. Just sat there readin' it and then readin' it again."

Davis nodded. "Good. Thanks," he told the ballplayer. Then he sought out the nearest Western Union office and sent a telegram.

The next stop for the barnstorming tour was Louisville. As the Barons came out of the dugout for batting practice that morning, Willie was surprised to hear his name being

32

called from the box seats behind first base. "Hey, Willie! Hey there, Willie!" He looked over searchingly. Then his eyes widened. He dropped the bat he had been holding and raced to the seats. "Aunt Sarah! Grandpa!" he called. He vaulted over the railing and into the box. "How—what are you doing here!" he exclaimed, hugging them.

"Well, Willie, we decided to put to good use some of that money you was sending us home," Aunt Sarah said. "So we came out to visit you and see how you were doing. Birmingham papers hardly write a word about this tour of yours."

His grandfather looked at him anxiously. "How *are* you doing, Willie?" he asked.

"Uh—great, Grandpa, just great. Been hitting the ball a mile. Couldn't Pop make the trip?"

"No, he couldn't get away from the mill. But he sends you his best thoughts, boy, and so do your ma and Mr. McMorris and all those stepbrothers and sisters of yours."

Willie grinned. "Gee, this sure is great, having both of you here to root for me. Just like the old days on the lots near the railroad yards, eh, Grandpa?"

"Yeah, just like it, Willie, only you ain't playin' for nickels and dimes now, boy. This is it. This is what we were talking about couple of years back when you graduated from Fairfield. I hope you realize that."

Aunt Sarah jabbed him sharply with her elbow. "Hush up, Grandfather Mays," she scolded. "Did you come here to hop on Willie and lecture him? If you did you can pack up and go home right now."

Willie chuckled delightedly. "Hot darn, Aunt Sarah, you haven't changed any, thank goodness. Still got a tongue sharp as fire."

"Only to them that needs it, Willie boy," she said. "Now your grandpa and me can only stay till tomorrow night, then we got to get back to Fairfield. So we got two whole games to see you play. Give us a treat to tell the folks back home, won't you, Willie?"

Willie grinned at her. "Aunt Sarah, I'll give you enough talk to keep you goin' till I get back home. Just you sit there and keep your eyes open. You, too, Grandpa," he said, poking the worried man in the stomach with his forefinger. "You watch ol' Willie show 'em how a Mays plays ball."

And Willie showed them. The first victim of his new determination was Don Newcombe, who had won seventeen games and lost eight that year for the Brooklyn Dodgers. His first time at bat Willie drove a double to left field. The next time Newcombe tried to scare him off with a brush back pitch that knocked him into the dirt. Willie got up, brushed himself off and hit Newcombe's next pitch right through the box for a single. On the first pitch to the next batter Willie took off for a try at stealing second. Roy Campanella, the All-Stars' catcher, whipped a throw to second baseman Jackie Robinson, but Willie hooked a slide around Robinson's tag and was safe.

In the Barons' dugout manager Piper Davis leaned out, looked over at Walter Mays and Aunt Sarah. Then he put his thumb and forefinger together to form a circle and waved it at them in the okay signal. Willie would be all right now.

For the rest of the tour Willie continued to batter All-Star pitching, confound the catching and frustrate the hitters with his amazing catches. Yet the net result was not that Willie attracted the attention of any major league scouts; their attention was focused instead on Lou Perry, the Barons' first baseman, who had had a barnstorming series no better than Willie's.

Perry's good fortune was that the manager of the Sioux City, Iowa, team of the Class A minor league was in desperate need of a first baseman. Since Sioux City was a farm team of the New York Giants, he appealed to them for help shortly after the opening of the 1950 season. He phoned Carl

Hubbell, chief of the Giants' farm system, who sent Ed Montague and Bill Harris after Lou Perry. The two men, veteran scouts for the Giants, were instructed to follow Perry's fortunes for a week and report back to Hubbell.

The scouts caught up with the Barons in Birmingham. They paid their way into the ball park and quietly took seats along the first base line to watch Perry. As the Barons took their infield practice before the game, Harris turned to Montague and shook his head. "Too old," he said.

"Yeah," the other scout agreed. "He's not bad, but there's no sense bringing a guy like Perry up to Class A ball." He sighed, stretched. "Well, shall we go home?"

Harris shrugged. "We're here, we might as well watch the ball game."

They sat back and relaxed as the umpire called "Play ball!" and the Barons took the field. By the sixth inning they were sitting on the edges of their seats, their arms resting on the railing, staring out at the field. Still neither man had said a word to each other. Then Bill Harris broke the silence. "Ed," he said, his voice tight, "do you see what I see?"

"Yeah, I see it all right," Montague breathed. "Only I'm not sure I believe it. I was sitting here hoping you'd say something first so I'd know it was true."

"What should we do?" Harris asked.

"I don't know yet. I'm afraid if we get up he'll go away or something. Maybe up in smoke like a magic genie for all I know."

"Maybe we should watch him a couple more days?"

Montague shook his head. "This kid's no freak. Not the way he moves out there. He knows what he's doing, all right. What's his name, anyway?"

"How should I know?" Harris said. "I came to look at Perry, same as you."

Montague whistled down a boy selling score cards and with his forefinger traced the names on the Barons' batting order. "Here he is, center fielder, Willie Mays." He looked over at Harris, shrugged. "Never heard of him. Did you?"

"No, and I hope nobody else has, either. Ed, I think we came to dig up iron and found gold."

Montague nodded. "Let's call Hubbell right away. For all we know there are nine other scouts sitting around here somewhere."

They left the ball park and drove rapidly away, looking for the first phone booth. They found one at a gas station and the two scouts squeezed into the booth together, pooled their silver and put through a call to the Giants' office in New York.

"Carl, we got a real live one for you," Harris said excitedly when Hubbell came on the wire.

"You mean Perry's good, eh?" the Giants' farm director asked.

"No, forget Perry, he's too old to start bringing up now. But listen, Carl, the Barons got a center fielder, a young kid, looks like a million bucks. Name's Willie Mays. Ever hear of him?"

Hubbell thought a moment. "Think I did once or twice. Monte Irvin mentioned his name around here, I think. So he's good, you say?"

"Good? Listen, Carl, you know me and Bill, we've been around long enough so we don't believe anything we hear and only half of what we see. Well, if this Mays is only half as good as we saw today then he's merely sensational, that's all."

"You talk to him?" Hubbell asked.

"We didn't talk to anybody. We just got out of there and called you right away."

"Okay, stay down there. I'll call Sioux City and call you later at your hotel."

Later that afternoon Hubbell's call came through. "Ed? This is Carl. Sioux City doesn't want this Mays kid."

"Doesn't want him!" Montague yelled. "What do they mean, they don't want him? What are they, crazy? I tell you this kid is going to be great, Carl!"

"I believe you, Ed," Hubbell said, "but Sioux City needs a first baseman, not an outfielder."

"Then the heck with Sioux City. Let them find their own first baseman. Let's try to place this kid somewhere before somebody else grabs him."

"You think he's that good?" Hubbell said, not quite convinced.

"Carl, I stake my reputation on it," Montague said soberly. "And Bill goes along with me on that."

"Okay then, hang by the phone and I'll see what I can do," Hubbell said.

An hour later he called back. "Got a spot for Mays," he said brightly. "Trenton. Interstate League. Sign the kid up."

IT CAME TOO SUDDENLY FOR WILLIE, THE JUMP FROM THE dream to the dream-come-true. Knowing in his heart that someday he would play in organized baseball—that was one thing. Actually signing a contract and donning a uniform— that was another. One day he was a center fielder for the Birmingham Barons, the next he was the center fielder for the Trenton farm team of the New York Giants—with a six-thousand-dollar bonus to boot. It was too much. He reported to Trenton in late June and didn't get a hit until July.

Fortunately for Willie's career, the Trenton general man- ager was Bill McKechnie, Jr., who was used to seeing jittery rookies come into the league. Twenty-two times Willie came up to bat in his first week with Trenton, and twenty-two times he was an easy out. Willie strained and sweated for a base hit; he tried to bunt his way on and place hits to right field. Neither strategy worked. As he pressed for a hit the strain began to tell on his fielding, until finally McKechnie took him aside and calmed him down. "I know it's easier to say than do," he said, "but calm down, Willie. You're acting like a two-year-old filly in her first race. Nobody expects you to tear the league apart your first time around."

"I gotta get a hit," Willie said anxiously.

"You'll get one, you'll get one," McKechnie soothed. "Just take it easy. Study the pitchers. Remember what they throw you. Watch where the fielders play you. The hits'll come, you'll see. You'll get a million of them before you're through."

But Willie shook his head. "I gotta get a hit," he repeated. It was the only cure for his nervousness.

On his twenty-third at-bat Willie broke the ice. He doubled against Willard Schmidt of the Allentown team his first time up. It was Willie's only hit of the game, but it was enough to shake off his youthful jitters. The next day he beat Allentown with a ninth inning home run and followed that with a seven-hit, three-game series against Wilmington that led Trenton to a sweep of the three games.

Willie came alive now. Loosened up, confident, he became the scourge of Interstate League pitching. One of his greatest days of that 1950 season was at the expense of the Sunbury team. On his first trip to the plate Willie doubled and promptly stole third. When the next Trenton batter flied out to deep right field, Willie tagged up and headed for home. He was halfway down the base line when his cap flew off. He stopped short, whirled, caught the cap in mid-air, whirled again and resumed his run for home. The fans were in a panic—as was McKechnie—but Willie made it home before the throw-in from the outfield.

In the third inning Trenton trailed, 3–2, but had men on first and third when Willie came up again. He let a bad curve go by, took a strike, then smacked the next pitch to right center field for a two-run double. Trenton's pitchers were having a bad day, however, and they lost the lead once more. In the sixth inning, when Willie came to bat for the third time, Sunbury was leading, 5–4. A Trenton runner was on first with a walk. Wasting no time, Willie jumped on the first pitch, sending it high and far to left field, over the outfielder's head and up against the wall nearly four hundred feet away. Willie never stopped running. He tore around the base paths like an express train. Rounding second his cap flew off again, but this time he didn't stop. He sped into third, got the go-ahead sign from his coach and turned for home. Ahead of him he saw the on-deck hitter with his hands spread low, a signal for Willie that he'd have to slide to make it. He put his head down and charged for the plate like a bull, saw the catcher set himself for the throw. Gauging the distance to the plate as he ran, Willie threw himself into a head-first slide, slamming into the catcher, bowling him over completely. "Safe!" called the plate umpire.

Willie's teammates jumped forward anxiously after the call, fearful that he had injured himself in the crash with the Sunbury catcher. But he jumped up grinning, dusted the dirt from his uniform and trotted into the dugout. The score was now 6–5, in favor of Trenton, and just to make sure, Willie homered in the eighth inning to make the final score 7–5.

In the Trenton clubhouse later, his teammates were ribbing Willie about his great exhibition of hitting and running, snapping towels at him in the shower, hiding his soap, loudly exclaiming to each other about how lucky that Mays was, the way his dinky little hits kept dropping in safely. The more Willie tried to get in a word of his own, the louder they talked, until he had to shout above the din to be heard. "Say-hey! Say-hey!" he yelled, trying to get their attention. "Those hits weren't lucky! Man, you see the way the ball took off on that homer!" he grinned, realizing that his teammates really were proud of him, were teasing him.

Game after game, as Willie's bat thundered up and down the east coast in the cities of the Interstate League, his teammates continued their horseplay. Not particularly gregarious by nature, Willie was nevertheless happy to make friends, and eagerly he went along with their joking. "Say-hey! Say-hey!" was heard continually in the Trenton locker room as Willie shouted for attention. "Did you see that catch I made out there today?" he would yell, deliberately egging them on to derision. "Lucky! Lucky!" would come the reply, and Willie would burst into laughter.

But the "Say-hey" stuck to Willie as a trade-mark. And "Say-hey" Willie Mays was born.

By the end of his season at Trenton Willie had the entire New York Giants organization watching him like a hungry sparrow eying a juicy worm. From President Horace Stoneham down to the lowliest clerk in the office, the word was "Willie Mays." The nineteen-year-old phenomenon hit .353 at Trenton, but the statistics couldn't record his circus catches, his amazing throws, his daring, colorful running on the base paths.

"Willie should play Triple-A ball next year," field manager Chick Genovese told the Giants, and Mays was promoted to the Minneapolis Millers for 1951. The Millers trained in Sanford, Florida, that spring, while the Giants were at St. Petersburg. One evening in March, after a Giant game in Orlando, manager Leo Durocher drove to Sanford to see what all the Willie Mays talk was about. The Millers' manager introduced them on the field just before game time. The two men shook hands and stood appraising each other silently. Then, simultaneously, each broke into a wide grin. "Hiya, Skip," was Willie's greeting. "Hiya, Willie," said Durocher. "I hear tell you're quite the boy. I came to see for myself. You gonna show me anything?"

Willie's grin grew wider. "Maybe. Maybe not. But don't turn around to buy a hot dog or anything 'cause you're liable to miss the best part."

Durocher laughed. As a New York sports writer later wrote, the meeting between Leo and Willie was "love at first sight."

The Giants' pilot took a seat behind the Millers' dugout

when the game began, and Willie obliged him by putting on a spectacular show. He singled, tripled and hit a home run in the ninth inning that won the game. Earlier, he had kept the contest within reach by making a catch on the dead run in deep center field, whirling and throwing out the runner coming down from third on a tag-up play.

Durocher returned to his hotel in Orlando raving about Willie. "The greatest! The greatest!" Leo exclaimed to all he could buttonhole in the hotel lobby. "The kid's got the greatest throwing arm, the greatest outfield range, the greatest bat I've ever seen on a player with his experience."

If there were skeptics among his listeners, it was understandable. Leo had a reputation for raving wildly about many ballplayers who later turned out to be a bust in the major leagues. Many a fizzle had started out as "the greatest" Leo had ever seen.

But Willie began the 1951 season justifying Durocher's most extravagant claims. The pitchers in the American Association couldn't get him out. He was batting .500 at the end of a month's play. The league hadn't seen anything like it since Ted Williams had played for the Millers in 1938, and Williams had hit only .366 that year in winning the batting championship. Fantastic stories began to drift to the Giants' office in New York. It was said that in Milwaukee the outfield fence had to be repaired after Willie hit three balls in a row against the boards. Pitchers who got Willie out once in a game considered themselves aces on the mound. The Giants sent out scout Hank DeBerry to check further on Mays, and what DeBerry came back with remains unmatched in the files of major league baseball. Normally, scouting reports are routine in language and description, laconically describing the pros and cons of a ballpayer. But DeBerry's report on Willie said this:

"Sensational. Is the outstanding player on the Minneapolis club and probably in all the minor leagues for that matter.

He is now on one of the most amazing hitting streaks imaginable. Hits all pitches and hits to all fields. Hits the ball where it is pitched as good as any player seen in many a day. Everything he does is sensational. He has made the most spectacular catches. Runs and throws with the best of them. Naturally, he has some faults, some of which are: he charges low-hit balls too much, sometimes runs with his head down. There have been a few times when his manager needed a rope, for when he starts somewhere he means to get there. Slides hard, plays hard. He is a marvel and just about as popular with the local fans as he can get. The Louisville pitchers knocked him down plenty but it seemed to have no effect on him at all. This player is the best prospect in America. It was a banner day for the Giants when this boy was signed."

In New York, Leo Durocher fairly drooled over the report. It not only vindicated his snap judgment of Mays; it brought news of possible help—something the Giants needed badly—and quickly. After a third place finish in 1950, they had strong hopes for a 1951 pennant, but the middle of May found them floundering around the edges of the first division. Durocher had a good infield, made up of Whitey Lockman on first, Eddie Stanky at second, Al Dark at shortstop and Hank Thompson—Willie's old rival from the Monarchs—on third. In the outfield there were Bobby Thomson, Monte Irvin and Don Mueller. Catching was Wes Westrum, pitching were Larry Jansen, Jim Hearn, Sal Maglie, Sheldon Jones and an assortment of others. It wasn't a bad line-up, but what it lacked was solid, reliable punch, and some spark to make the whole team move.

Leo Durocher looked at scout Hank DeBerry's report and knew he had that punch, that spark. He took the report into President Stoneham's office, dropped it on his desk. "I want Mays," he said, pointing at the paper.

Stoneham looked pained. "Not now. Not yet, Leo."

"Why not now?" Leo growled. "I need him. The Giants need him."

"So do the Millers," Stoneham parried. "Besides, Mays is the most popular player they ever had out there. They'd lynch us if we took him away now."

"So who's more important, the Minneapolis fans or the Giant team?" Durocher demanded.

Stoneham squirmed. "Wait a few more days, Leo. Let's see what happens."

Leo glared at him a moment, then turned and stalked out. But each day, as the Giants continued to stall and the Dodgers opened up a wider lead over the league, Durocher reminded Stoneham of the phenomenon in Minneapolis. "When, Horace, when?" he needled, and Stoneham answered, "Soon, Leo, soon." Until finally he could hold out no longer. The Giants needed some kind of shot in the arm, and Willie Mays looked like it. Resignedly, Stoneham gave Durocher the word he had been waiting for. "Okay, Leo, get him," he said.

Durocher's eyes widened. "Mays?" he asked.

Stoneham nodded. "I know in advance what the reaction in Minneapolis will be, so I've arranged to take a full-page ad in the papers there, explaining our position. Still, I don't think it will be safe for either of us in Minneapolis for years to come."

Durocher whooped with joy. "The devil with Minneapolis. Watch us move now!" He grabbed the telephone off Stoneham's desk and placed a call to the Millers' hotel in Minneapolis. Willie wasn't in. "Find him for me!" Leo yelled to the operator in Minneapolis. "This is Leo Durocher calling him from New York. It's important!"

"I'll try to locate Mr. Mays for you, sir," the operator said. "I'll phone you if I find him."

"I'll be right here. Call me, no matter when it is. I won't go away from the phone."

So popular and well known was Willie in Minneapolis that in half an hour the operator had traced him to a local movie theater. When she got through to the theater manager and explained what the call was about, he stopped the film and stepped out on stage. "There's a phone call for Willie Mays from New York," he announced proudly. "Willie, you can take it in my office."

Embarrassed, Willie rose from his seat in the theater and sheepishly walked to the manager's office while the movie patrons applauded and cheered. All knew what an urgent phone call from New York meant.

Willie picked up the phone gingerly. "Hello?" he said.

"This is Leo, Willie. Leo Durocher! Listen, Willie, pick up a ticket, grab a plane and meet us in Philadelphia tomorrow."

Suddenly Willie's body turned cold. He just stared into the phone's mouthpiece, unable to answer. "Willie! Willie!" he heard the voice on the other end. "Willie, do you hear me!"

He gulped. "You're making a mistake, Skip," he said. "You don't want me."

"What are you talking about!" Durocher roared across two thousand miles of wire. "Of course I want you! You're just the man I need!"

"No! No!" Willie backed away from the phone. "No, I tell you you're making a mistake! I'm not good enough, Skip, you don't want me!"

"Willie," Durocher snapped, "what are you hitting?"

"Four seventy-seven," he confessed.

"And you still think I don't need you? Willie, grab that plane and be in Philadelphia tomorrow—or I'll come out there and get you!"

Willie heaved a long sigh. "Yes, Skip, I'll do it. I'll be there. Philadelphia. Tomorrow." He cradled the phone slowly and stared at the grinning face of the theater manager.

"Philadelphia. Tomorrow," he said. "Philadelphia. Tomorrow," he repeated, over and over again as he walked out of the theater and headed for the hotel to pack his bags.

5

In the visitors' dressing room at Shibe Park, Philadelphia, the New York Giants quietly changed into their gray road uniforms. Desultory conversation and the clanging metal of locker doors was the theme of sound that traveled with the Giants. There was little to be gay about; they were not an ebullient group of players to begin with, and their eleven-game losing streak in April and fifth place rut dampened what little flavor for merriment they might have had.

Then, on that evening of May 25th, Willie Mays squeezed sideways through the dressing room entrance, a battered suitcase in his left hand, a golf bag with three bats in it slung over his right shoulder. He looked around the dressing room wide eyed for a moment. Several of the Giants looked back at him appraisingly. Then Willie grinned widely. "Say-hey!" he said brightly, "my name is Willie Mays. Is Mr. Leo Durocher here?"

Eddie Stanky looked at Willie, then turned and looked at Al Dark—and smiled. Dark looked at Willie, turned to Sal Maglie—and grinned. Somehow, as Willie stood there in the doorway, his twenty-year-old's innocence showing all over his face, smiles and grins—and somewhere in the room a low chuckle—became very much in evidence. Shortstop Dark, an excellent golfer, strode to the doorway and felt Willie's golf bag. "Nice stuff," he said amiably. "What do you go around in, Willie?"

Willie's grin remained, but his eyes were suddenly vacant. "Go around in?" He wasn't sure that this man—he didn't know who Dark was by sight—wasn't kidding him about something.

"Yeah," Dark explained. "You know, what's your usual golf score?"

Willie breathed a sigh of relief. "Oh, I never played golf. That's a rich man's game."

There were more chuckles around the dressing room. Monte Irvin, Stanky, Bobby Thomson and Whitey Lockman crowded around Mays. "Then what's the golf bag for?" Dark asked.

"Oh, that!" Willie laughed loudly. "Some nice folks in Minneapolis gave it to me for a going-away present. Makes a dandy bat holder, don't it?" He looked around the group for approval.

A figure, shorter than most, elbowed his way through. "All right, all right, break it up, what's goin' on here?" the raspy voice of Leo Durocher broke in. He stopped short in front of Willie. "Hey! Willie! You got here!"

"Sure I did, Mr. Leo. I still say you're making a big mistake, but I got here, just like I told you I would."

Durocher turned to the Giant players. "Fellas, I want you all to meet Willie Mays, 'cause he's goin' to be around these parts for a long, long time. Irvin, you take him under your wing and teach him the ropes. He'll room with you on the road." He turned back to Willie. "Got a uniform all ready for you, kid. Number twenty-four. Like it?"

Willie shrugged. "Numbers don't mean nothing to me, Mr. Leo. All I worry about is playing ball. If I'm playing ball, I'm happy."

Durocher nodded and patted him on the back. "Get dressed, kid. And from now on, don't you worry about nothing. I'll do all the worrying for you. You just get up there and take your cuts." To the other players he called, "Let's go, let's go, batting practice in five minutes! There's gonna be some changes around here now!"

Willie was one of the last to emerge on the playing field. He blinked momentarily as he stepped out under the bright lights of the park, then walked to the bat rack, selected one of the three that the bat boy had taken from the golf bag and stored with the rest. Durocher walked over to him, put his arm around his shoulders. "Stay loose, kid. You nervous?"

Willie nodded.

"You'll get over it soon as the game starts. Uh, one thing though, Willie. You know, some of the pitchers are gonna be throwing at you. Trying to scare you away from the plate . . ."

"I expect that, Mr. Leo," Willie replied quietly. "They threw at me all over. But the way I figure it, they got to throw some of 'em good enough to hit, and then—wham!—I show 'em I ain't scared."

Durocher smiled, squeezed Willie's arm and returned to his place on the bench. Willie got in line, waiting his turn at batting practice. Wes Westrum was in the cage, followed by Hank Thompson and Stanky. They each took their swings, ran out the final bunt, then Willie stepped in to the batter's box. Every man in Giant uniform focused his attention on the plate. Durocher leaned forward anxiously on the bench. The other Giants in the dugout continued to lounge carelessly, but the tension was felt all along the line of expectant players.

Willie dug in at the plate. The pitch came down. He swung. The ball leaped from the bat, darted in a high line to left field and plunked into the left field seats.

48

Something that sounded like a long sigh came from the Giant bench.

Willie continued his batting practice swings. Solid line drives sprayed from his bat like water jetting from a hose. Two more drives landed in the left stands before he was through. On his last swing, as was customary, he bunted and raced for first base. Halfway down the base line his cap flew off. Without breaking stride he caught it in mid-air and beat the third baseman's throw to first. Chuckling, Willie turned and trotted back to the bench. "Hey, Mr. Leo, I hit a couple good, didn't I?" he said.

Durocher stared at him innocently. "You did? Say, I guess I forgot to look."

Willie burst into loud laughter. "Say-hey! You kiddin' me, Mr. Leo! I saw you watching me!" Still laughing, he picked his glove off the bench and ran out on the grass for his outfield practice.

Just before game time that evening Durocher handed the line-up to the plate umpire. Stanky led off and played second base, then came first baseman Lockman, Willie batted third and played center field, third baseman Hank Thompson batted fourth, followed by Westrum, Irvin, Dark, Thomson and pitcher Jim Hearn. Pitching for the Phillies would be Bubba Church.

Finally the groundskeepers smoothed out the infield, the national anthem was played and the plate umpire called "Play ball!" for Willie Mays's first major league baseball game.

Church disposed of Stanky and Lockman easily, then Willie stepped in to hit. The Philadelphia pitcher was well aware of the rookie's reputation and his .477 batting average at Minneapolis; but this was the major leagues, not Triple-A ball. Church reared back and threw a strike past Willie's flailing bat.

The next pitch was outside, for ball one. In the third base

49

coaching box, Leo Durocher paced like a caged tiger, trying to hide his own anxiety from the youngster at the plate. Church leaned down, got the sign, spun a curve ball over that Willie took for called strike two. Willie stepped out of the batter's box, stooped, got a handful of dirt and rubbed it between his palms, stepped back in. Church threw a fast ball low. Willie lunged, checked in time. Ball two—two balls and two strikes on him now.

On the mound, Church drew a deep breath. He squinted for the sign, wound up, threw a curve—it broke sharply and over the plate. Willie looked at it—and it was called strike three! He turned disgustedly and stomped away from the plate. Durocher called to him from the coach's box, "Never mind there, Willie boy, the next one'll be yours, kid!"

The next one for Willie came in the third inning. This time he grounded meekly to the second baseman and was thrown out at first. In the fifth inning he flied out. In the seventh inning the Giants were trailing, 5–2, with two out, when, with Dark on first, Stanky and Lockman singled to drive in a run and put the tying runs on the bases. Again Willie stepped up to hit. Grimly, he planted his spikes in the dirt and swung on Church's first pitch. The ball leaped from his bat and soared to deep left field. Dick Sisler, the Philadelphia left fielder, turned and raced for the wall, backed up against it, leaped—and speared Willie's drive with one hand for the third out.

In the next inning the Giants drove Church out with a five-run rally that won the game, 8–5. In his fifth at bat for the day, Willie grounded out, ending the eighth inning rally.

When the game was over, he trotted in from the outfield and morosely began to undress. Monte Irvin slapped a wet towel at him and laughed. "Hey, we pulled that game out of the fire, eh, Willie?" And several of the other players stopped by as he undressed to shake his hand and mutter, "Nice goin', Willie." Manager Durocher caught him in the shower

50

and yelled, "You looked good out there, Willie kid, you looked good!"

Willie was grateful for the words of encouragement. He felt a warmth inside that told him these men, these strangers, were his friends. But the warmth lasted only a moment. Then the coldness came again, the coldness that told him he had played badly, had looked like the raw busher he was. He gulped back the tears, finished showering, dressed in his street clothes and went out to the bus that would take the Giants back to their hotel. Irvin, his roommate, climbed aboard soon afterward and took a seat beside him. Monte knew what was boiling inside the frightened youngster. He took a couple of western paperbacks out of his overnight case and handed one to Willie. "Tomorrow's another day, Willie. There's plenty of hits in your bat. We all know that."

Willie nodded dumbly. He opened the pages of a book and pretended to read, but the words were a blur. When the other players began trooping onto the bus, he closed his eyes and pretended he was asleep.

The next afternoon, behind the pitching of Larry Jansen, the Giants beat the Phillies again, 2–0. Again Willie failed to hit; he came up five times, made out three and walked twice. His spirits continued to sink, though the Giants ignored his brief failure to hit, buoyed by two successive wins that brought them to the .500 mark in won-lost percentage for the first time since the 1951 season's opening week. In the field, at least, though he had had no occasion to demonstrate anything spectacular, Willie played smoothly and professionally, covering center field perfectly.

But this wasn't enough for him. He knew that Durocher had brought him up to the Giants primarily for his batting prowess, not his fielding. When he went hitless again on the third straight day, the fact that the Giants won their third straight was of no comfort to him. After that game at Philadelphia, the Giants entrained for home; there was a night game scheduled against the Braves for the next day, and ace Warren Spahn was due to oppose them. As the train clacked over the rails, Willie sat with his elbow on the window sill, staring out at the red rays of the dying sun. Farther down the car, manager Durocher watched him narrowly.

The Polo Grounds was packed with a noisy crowd the following evening. Despite the fact that Willie had gone twelve times without a hit—or perhaps even because of it—there was a host of the curious and the disbelieving on hand. Long-suffering Giant fans had seen one alleged star after another during the managerial days of Mel Ott and the first two full years of Leo Durocher's reign. None of the supposed "phenoms" had worked out. Was Willie Mays another second-rater inflated by the Giants' publicity men? Judged by his first three games, it certainly looked that way to the fans. But they were on hand nevertheless to see the newest wonder unveiled at home.

At the moment, the subject of their wonder sat alone in the locker room of the Giants. His teammates already had gone on the field for pregame practice. But Willie had dressed slowly; even now, as he sat on a stool in front of his locker, his head buried in his hands, he wore only his base-ball pants and sweat shirt. His Number 24 shirt hung before him in the open locker.

On the field, Leo Durocher looked around him curiously. He walked up to Irvin. "Seen Willie?" he asked. Irvin looked around, shrugged. "I thought I saw him come out. Maybe he's still getting dressed." Durocher nodded. "Yeah, maybe." He squinted into the bright lights, peering into the outfield. No Willie. "Hey, Sal," he walked over to pitcher Maglie, "you see Willie out here?" Maglie thought a moment, then shook his head. Durocher looked around once more, then ducked into the passageway that led under the stands and walked quickly to the Giants' clubhouse.

He opened the door softly and peered in. There was Willie, sitting alone in the pale glow of a naked light bulb overhead, his head still bowed in his hands. He looked up, startled at the sound of spiked shoes clattering on concrete. Durocher's heart wrenched at the sight of the tear-streaked face that turned up to him, the eyes, lost and frightened and pleading. Leo pulled over a stool and sat down next to him. "What's eatin' you, kid?" he said softly.

The words poured out in a rush. "Oh, I told you, Mr. Leo, I told you I wasn't good enough to play here!" Willie rocked back and forth, sobbing aloud. "Didn't I tell you that time on the telephone, didn't I tell you I wasn't good enough! You made me come here! You made me!"

Leo sighed, rubbed his jaw with his fingers. "What are you talking about, Willie, you're not good enough? That's no kind of talk from a man like you. Why, you're the best!"

"No I'm not! You can't kid me with that talk any more, Mr. Leo. Look at me. Not a hit yet in three games!" Willie buried his face again. "Please, Mr. Leo, please send me back to Minneapolis!"

Durocher gulped hard. He put his arm around the youngster's heaving shoulders. "Willie. Now, Willie, I want you to listen to me. And listen to me good. You're gonna get your hits soon. You're too good to miss. But I want you to know this, and remember it from now on. You're my center fielder even if you never get a hit. Never! Because you're the greatest fielder I ever saw. Hear me, Willie! You're the greatest. Remember I played with and saw some of the best, but you're better than any of them—Terry Moore, DiMaggio, Snider, Musial. You're better than any of them. And you're my boy, hits or no hits."

Leo stood up. "I'm going back on the field now, Willie. Come on out soon. The fans are waiting to see you take your batting practice cuts." He hesitated a moment, watched as Willie's sobs quieted, then turned and walked out of the

53

locker room. Outside, in the dim passageway that led to the dugout, he took a handkerchief from his pocket and blew his nose. Then, drawing a deep breath, he was ready to go out to the field.

Five minutes later Willie emerged, unsmiling but clear eyed. Durocher studiously avoided him for the rest of the practice session. When the game began, wordlessly Leo patted him on the back as he trotted out to his center field position. On the bench, Sal Maglie said, "What do you think, Skip? Think he'll be all right?"

Durocher set his lips tightly. "He'll be great."

Still batting third in the line-up, Willie came up to hit in the first inning with the Giants trailing, 3–0, the Braves having knocked out Sheldon Jones in their turn at bat. Spahn, one of the most competent pitchers in the National League, retired Stanky and Lockman, then set about pitching to Willie. The lean left-hander threw a curve in for a strike. The next two pitches were outside; the count was two balls and a strike.

Spahn picked up the signal from his catcher Del Crandall, wound up, kicked high with his right leg, came down with a fast ball across the letters. Willie dug in with his spikes and swung. There was a solid crack that jerked the crowd to its feet. The ball sailed high and far toward left field. The Braves' fielder ran back a few steps, then stopped and watched helplessly as the ball soared up and over the left field roof for a home run.

The Giant players leaped off the bench and cheered. Durocher, doing a little dance in the third base coaching box, shook his fist in the air and yelled to no one in particular, "Did I tell ya! Did I tell ya!" The crowd stood up and roared its approval at the tremendous power of the homer. Pitcher Spahn took off his cap, mopped his brow with his shirt sleeve and stared in wonder at the youngster gracefully circling the bases.

Willie, a contented grin on his face, trotted around the base paths, feeling the surge of reassurance well up inside of him and spread through his body, giving wings to his feet and breath to his lungs. He rounded third and gripped the extended hand of his manager Leo Durocher, then cantered toward home plate as the applause and the cheers from the fans spread and grew louder. He tipped his cap in acknowledgment as he crossed the plate and was greeted with the outstretched hands of his teammates. He walked back to the dugout; his back was straight, his face peaceful.

6

BUT IT WASN'T OVER YET FOR WILLIE MAYS IN THOSE DARK days of early 1951. He had won one battle with his homer off Spahn; there still was another war to be won. The war with himself, with his own insecurity.

The Giants lost the game, 4–1, and Willie went hitless his next three at-bats. Neither did he get a hit in the double-header against the Braves the following day, nor against the Pirates the day after that.

The home run was his only hit in his first twenty-six times at bat.

Self-doubt returned to Willie. It began with that burning emptiness in the hollow of his stomach as he stepped into the batter's box, spread like an inexorable tide of molten lava through his body, seared finally into his brain.

I'm no good! I'm no good! His mind throbbed with the anguish. At first fiercely, then resignedly, brokenly, he fought the pressure. Futilely he waved his bat at what seemed an unfathomable succession of fast balls and curves served by nameless supermen. He was ready to break.

Leo Durocher had been watching him covertly. The wise skipper of the Giants, for all his flamboyant gruffness, knew young ballplayers; perhaps he knew Willie best of all. He wrestled with Willie's problem and thought he saw a solution. But with the solution came another problem: How to present it to Willie without confirming his conviction that he was a failure? How to keep the cure from being more immediately fatal than the disease?

"Willie," Durocher said to him before the next day's game, "I want you to do me a favor." He looked embarrassed as he said it.

"Me? Do you a favor?" Willie's eyes widened.

"Yeah. You see, I'm in kind of a spot. I hate to ask a guy like you to do it, but you're really the only one I could count on for the job."

"What is it, Mr. Leo? You know I'd help you do anything if I could."

Durocher nodded. "Look, I'll fill you in on the situation. We're beginning to move up, come alive. We got a chance to break out and catch the Dodgers. But I got a dead spot in the batting order that kills a lot of rallies right in the middle. I need you to fill in that dead spot, make it so that the pitchers don't get a chance to ease up and get out of trouble, you know what I mean?"

Willie shook his head. "Not exactly, Mr. Leo. I don't see where I'll be doing you any favors. I ain't hittin' worth a nickel."

"Let me finish. You see, this dead spot is the eighth spot in the batting order. Now every time we get a rally going by the middle of the batting order, up comes Westrum, in eighth place, and the pitcher. Boom! The end of the rally. Westrum is a good catcher, but he's never gonna win any hitting medals. Now I figure if I put a clouter like you batting eighth, the pitcher isn't gonna get two easy outs in a row. He'll get the pitcher, but before that he's got to bear down on you, then after that the top of the order comes up again."

Willie nodded now. "I get it, Mr. Leo."

"Good. Now like I said, I know it isn't fair maybe to ask a guy like you to hit in the eighth spot, but if you would go along with me awhile on it, I'd sure appreciate it, Willie."

"Sure thing, Mr. Leo," Willie said, and Durocher thought he detected a trace of enthusiasm in his voice. "Tell you the truth, the way I've been going, I shouldn't be hitting third anyways. Maybe hitting down there will be helping both of us."

Durocher chucked him with his knuckles across the chin. "Atta boy, Willie. I knew you wouldn't let me down." He turned away and went out into the sunshine; it somehow seemed brighter. Maybe Willie wasn't that ingenuous, he thought. Maybe Willie suspected that his skipper's strategy was to get him out of the third spot in the batting order, where the pressure was greatest, down to the weaker eighth position, where he might catch an opposing pitcher easing up. Maybe Willie did suspect, but he couldn't be sure, not the way the proposition was presented. Even if the kid were suspicious, he might be relieved to be demoted to a less prominent position, at the same time saving face.

So on June 1st Willie was dropped to eighth in the batting order. His first time up, in the third inning, he banged a solid line drive single to center field, and came around moments later to score the Giants' first run of the game. But by the sixth inning the Pirates, leading, 3–2, had a rally going with two men on base and Ralph Kiner at bat. Jim Hearn, the Giant pitcher, threw the Pirates' top slugger a fast ball. Kiner hit the ball so hard he grunted at the impact. The ball soared like a missile to deepest left center field. Willie turned his back on home plate and sped toward the bleachers. Off came his cap—he grabbed at it with his bare hand, caught it without losing stride, and the crowd roared. They roared still louder a moment later as Willie, running full speed ahead, charged at the bleacher wall near the 440-foot mark, leaped and caught the drive with his back against the wall.

It was one of the longest drives ever hit—and caught—in the Polo Grounds.

Willie loped into the Giant dugout after the catch, applause and cheers ringing in his ears. He met Durocher coming off the bench. "Say-hey, Mr. Leo!" he grinned. "You see that catch?"

Durocher grinned back at him. "My grandmother could have done it."

Willie nearly bent double with laughter.

In the seventh inning, with one out and the Giants still trailing by one run, Al Dark tripled and held third as Irvin beat out a roller to the infield. Up stepped Willie. Pitcher Paul LaPalme curved him for a strike, then threw a fast ball. Willie swung, hit the pitch virtually to the same spot Kiner had hit his, but no Pirate outfielder could come close to it; the ball ricocheted off the bleacher wall untouched. Dark trotted home, Irvin scoring behind him, and Willie made it standing up to third base for a triple. The Giants took over the lead, 4–3.

Willie's resounding hit knocked LaPalme out of the box. Jim Walsh replaced him. But by this time it was too late. The Giants' spirit, long smoldering, needed just that touch of the torch provided by Willie's catch and his triple. Before the inning was over, six runs crossed the plate; the final score was Giants fourteen, Pirates three, and the Giants were just three percentage points out of third place.

Willie began his move, and with him moved the Giants. He hit safely in ten straight games; important hits that drove in runs and won ball games. A two-run double in the eighth inning beat the Reds for Sal Maglie, 3–2. A home run was good for three runs and a 6–4 victory over the Phillies. In Chicago a 6–6 tie went briefly into the tenth inning. Then Cub pitcher Dutch Leonard gave up singles to Whitey Lockman and Ray Noble. Willie came up next and hit Leonard's first pitch—his famous knuckleball—for a home run that broke open the game.

There was a new sound to be heard in the locker room of the New York Giants. Above the clanging of locker doors and the hissing spray of showers there was laughter; laughter deep, vigorous, and high pitched—the laughter of Willie Mays and his teammates. And there came a frequent "Say-hey!" as Willie, excited, shrilly tried to get attention to tell a story or protest some horseplay directed at him. He was slapped at with wet towels; buckets of cold water were emptied at him as he showered; his shoelaces were frayed thin so that they broke when he tried to tie them; once he was locked in an empty storage room under the stands at Shibe Park until he laughingly begged for mercy.

On June 25th Willie hit a home run and a double and Maglie shut out the Dodgers, 4–0, to lift the Giants to second place in the National League pennant race. A reporter for a New York newspaper wrote, "Giant fans, so long without hope, are chanting a new litany these days: 'Willie Mays is here; all's right with the world.' "

Mays was electric, there was no question about it. When the Giants were trailing in a ball game, you could feel it in the stands, hear it spoken and buzzed through the crowd: "Willie's up next inning. We ain't dead yet. Willie'll pull it out, you'll see." Veteran baseball writers discounted much of the fans' worship, but amazing to behold was the same effect on the Giant players themselves. They could be seen stirring on the bench in the late innings, waiting for Willie to come to bat, confident he would start something.

In July manager Durocher told Milton Gross of the New York *Post*, "Willie is the best rookie I ever saw. I wouldn't trade him for Musial, DiMaggio, Williams—or anybody."

Gross raised an eyebrow skeptically.

"That's right," Durocher insisted. "Willie's only twenty, but he's the greatest all-round player in the league. He's got a great batting eye, terrific power, a fantastic throwing arm, great fielding judgment, speed afoot and quick savvy. He's given us a tremendous lift since joining the club."

The road ahead appeared clear for Willie; the skies blue and bright. But there were storm clouds on the horizon. Fortunately for him, he had Leo Durocher backing him up.

There was a day in midsummer when, baseball cap in hand, head bowed in embarrassment, Willie came to his manager and asked to speak to him in private. "Come into the office." Durocher guided him into the manager's cubicle near the clubhouse. "Sit down," he said, but Willie remained standing, twisting his cap in his hands.

"Mr. Leo," he said finally, "I got a bad problem. You know I ain't the kind of boy that's bothered by those bench jockeys. I just don't hear them. But they've been calling out some bad things lately, and giving me the business on the bases sometimes."

"What kind of bad things, Willie?" Durocher asked quietly.

Willie shifted his feet, bit his lip. "You know, about my race, things like that." He lifted his eyes and thrust out his jaw defiantly. "I don't like that, Mr. Leo. That ain't no way to be kidding around."

"No, it isn't, Willie."

Willie's voice broke a little. "I don't know what to do about it, Mr. Leo. I don't want to make no trouble. I don't want people to think I got a chip on my shoulder. But I don't like that kind of name calling!"

"No, I'll bet you don't Willie," Leo said gently. He leaned back in his chair a moment, closed his eyes, then opened them, leaning forward across his desk. "I'll tell you what I think you should do," said Durocher, who had been preparing for this day he knew must come. "I think you should get deaf."

"Get deaf!" Willie stared at him.

61

Durocher nodded. "You see, Willie, some of those guys who've been calling you names, slurring your race, they're just stupid. They don't even mean it. Some of the other guys do mean it, of course. But all of them have two things in common. They're jealous because you're better than they are, and they're trying to get you so mad you'll make mistakes. Now, if you let them get under your skin and you fight back, blow your top, they'll just smirk to each other and say, 'What I tell ya, they can't take it.' You want that to happen?"

"No, Mr. Leo. But—"

"Never mind the 'buts.' I tell you from experience. Don't you think this happened to Monte Irvin, to Thompson, to Campanella and Newcombe? And how about Jackie Robinson? Remember this, Willie. If you were no good as a player, these guys wouldn't waste their time on you. But the better you are, the more they try to shake you up. And you—you're the best. And you gotta show these guys you're the best. Not only the way you play ball, but the way you act as a man. Show them you're better than they are by ignoring them. You'll see. After a while they'll cut it out."

Durocher got up and walked around the desk, putting his arm around Willie's shoulders. "There's bad guys wherever you go, Willie," he said. "Think of the good guys all around you. They're what count."

Willie put his cap back on, sighing deeply. "You talk sense, Mr. Leo. It's gonna be hard, but I'll do what you tell me. From now on—Willie, he don't hear nothin'."

Throughout the summer, true to his word, Willie heard nothing—except the cheers of the crowds and Durocher's continued ecstatic statements about him to the press. Each great fielding play, every vital hit and home run was an occasion for Leo to expound to the press about how great Willie was. Until, early in August, one of the sports writers cornered him in the clubhouse and told him his raves about Willie were on the verge of causing trouble.

"I hear things you don't," the writer told him. "The players talk when I'm around, even talk to me where they won't talk to you. And some of the guys are beginning to resent the way you're laying it on about Willie."

"Which guys?" Durocher demanded.

"Never mind which guys. I'm just telling you, Leo, you're only making it bad for Willie by sounding off about him all the time."

"But don't those guys understand why I'm doing it?" Durocher said.

"Understand what?" the reporter asked.

"Gee, I figured they'd get it, but if you don't either—I guess I figured because I knew Willie so well, everybody else did, too."

"What does that mean?"

Durocher sighed. "You see, it's like this. There are some ballplayers, you have to be tough on them, especially when they're slumping. You got to threaten them, yell at them, bench them even, to keep them on the ball. Other guys you got to go easy on, coax them, encourage them, kid them along. Willie, he's an extreme example of the second kind of player. He's a kid, he's colored, he's scared and he's inexperienced. Altogether he played maybe a hundred games in organized baseball before he came here. That's a big jump for anybody. For a kid with a background like Willie's it's like jumping to a mountaintop. He made it, but now that he's there he's afraid he'll fall right off. So Willie I got to tell he's the greatest, over and over again. And I got to tell it to other guys so Willie'll hear me. Holler at Willie when he's down and he'll sink right to the bottom."

The sports writer stared at Durocher with new respect. "Leo, I've been covering this league a lot of years. I always thought you were a pretty good manager, but a big mouth. I'd like to shake your hand."

"Aah, get out of here," Durocher said, embarrassed.

The reporter grinned. "I'm glad I spoke to you first, anyway, before I printed anything. I wouldn't have wanted Willie to see it."

"I don't think Willie bothers to read what you guys write. He's too smart."

The reporter laughed. "Listen, Leo, you want me to tell the players what you said about Willie, explain to them?"

"No. I think that's something I better do myself." Durocher thanked the reporter for tipping him off to the impending trouble, left the clubhouse and walked out onto the field. He had a fair idea of who the complaining players were, but to make certain he covered them all, and to avoid singling out any group, he went from player to player before that day's game, speaking quietly, explaining the reasons behind his continual extravagant praising of Willie. The grumbling disappeared.

Unaware of the drama acted out behind him, of his manager's psychological weaning of him, Willie continued his sparking of the ball club. His terrible start weighed down his batting average, but by August he had raised it to a respectable .275. The figure was deceptive. There were things he did that defied statistics—his incredible fielding, his bubbling good nature that gave the entire team a lift in its struggling moments, the hits that began a rally, that upset a pitcher, the personal oddities that gave his teammates a laugh, made them exclaim, "That Willie! He's a card!" and sent them out to play refreshed and with renewed spirit.

The Giants were locked in a struggle for second place, and just when things were grimmest, the tension its tautest, Willie would make one of his peculiar patented catches, as though he were catching peaches in a bushel basket held at his waist, or he would get a hit and in rounding the bases his cap would fly off, and he would stop to retrieve it before going on—without missing a base.

And the Giants would laugh and relax—and win.

64

Suddenly, on August 13th, the Giants stopped and looked around. They were alone in second place. Below them the enemy had been vanquished; above them, leading by thirteen games, were the Dodgers—untouchable, breezing toward the pennant. The race was apparently over. The next day the Dodgers invaded the Polo Grounds, determined to finish off the Giants' chances for good.

The Giants beat them in the opening game of the series, 4–2, but there were still twelve games separating the two teams. The Dodgers threw Ralph Branca against Jim Hearn the following afternoon, trying to regain the lost ground. Time was on their side; the season was running out. Now all they had to do was maintain an even pace to win the pennant, while the Giants could not afford to lose a single game.

Through seven innings Branca and Hearn dueled in a 1–1 tie. But with one out in the eighth inning, Billy Cox stood on third base and Carl Furillo stepped into the batter's box. A fly ball was all that was needed to score Cox and put the Dodgers ahead. Furillo, a dangerous right-handed hitter, dug in at the plate. Willie shifted toward left center field, the proper spot for Furillo. But Carl hit one of Hearn's pitches to deep right center, and Willie was off at the crack of the bat.

On third, Cox played it cautiously. He had seen Willie in action before, so though the ball looked like a hit, he held up at third. Even if by some miracle Willie did catch the ball, he could tag up at third and score easily after the catch. So Cox watched carefully as Willie, running out from under his cap, stretched out at the last moment and caught the ball on the run, headed for right center field, away from the plate. Cox tagged up and raced for home. Whitey Lockman moved off first base onto the outfield grass near second to take the throw in, conceding the run to Cox, as did catcher Westrum, who crouched at home plate just to give Cox a run for his money.

But Willie conceded nothing. As he caught the ball, running full speed to his right, he wheeled completely around to his left and, in the same motion, lined up his sights on home plate and heaved. The ball sailed high over Lockman's head and thumped into Westrum's mitt. Cox, sliding in, was tagged out.

For a moment there was stunned silence in the Polo Grounds. Then a roar erupted as the realization of what they had witnessed hit the fans. On the field the players came out of their shock, too, with mixed reactions. Cox stood at home plate, bewildered, not believing that Willie had actually caught him. Furillo, himself the possessor of a reputation as the finest arm in the league, stared out toward center field in awe. The rest of the Dodgers, numbed with shock, slowly came out of it and walked dejectedly to their positions as the Giants trotted into the dugout. On the bench his teammates pummeled Willie with glee.

"That was the perfectest throw I ever made," he said proudly, and for once Leo Durocher was at a loss for a humorous retort.

Once again an outstanding play by Willie sparked the Giants. Spurred on by the incredible throw, they came to bat in their half of the eighth inning determined to make it pay off. Willie led off with a single, and a few moments later trotted across the plate ahead of Westrum's home run, and the Giants had pulled the game out of the fire, 3–1.

The victory was a tremendous jolt in the arm for the Giants, but it was mid-August, and they still trailed the Dodgers by eleven games. Nobody on the team dared utter the thought out loud, but day by day the hope flashed brighter into the minds of the Giant players. Quietly, they ran their winning streak to six games, to eight games, to ten, and even the Giant fans began to stir with interest. Sixteen straight games the Giants won, and suddenly they were only six games behind the Dodgers.

Now the pressure shifted to the Brooklyn team. They had

held a seemingly insurmountable lead, had been expected to win the pennant; if they held off the Giants, they would simply be doing what had been predicted for them. If they lost it now, they would be known forever as the team that "blew" the pennant.

On the other hand, the Giants played loosely. It was miracle enough that they were in second place, offering the Dodgers a challenge. They continued to chip away the Dodgers' lead—six games to five, to four, to three, back to four, then three again. Then the teams were only two games apart—and the last week of the season at hand. Now all New York City concentrated on the battle. Perhaps for the first time baseball fans seriously considered that the Giants had a chance to win the pennant. For the first time they saw the real miracle in the Giants' long uphill fight.

The Dodgers' lead shrank to one game. Then they led by two again. Then one. Then they were tied—with two games left to go! The Giants had their final game at Boston, the Dodgers at Philadelphia. In their first games at Boston, the Giants pitted Sal Maglie against Warren Spahn. For two innings the game was scoreless. Then, with one out in the third, Willie singled. He took his lead off first, fidgeting impatiently as the Braves' pitcher threw a ball and a strike past Wes Westrum. Willie had stolen only five bases all year, but he felt that the time was ripe for another attempt. He wanted desperately to get into scoring position, realizing the vital nature of each little opportunity gained against a pitcher like Spahn.

He watched carefully as the Boston star stretched, threw to the plate. It was strike two. Willie felt that Spahn would waste the next pitch, try to get Westrum to hit at a bad ball. It would be high or low, maybe inside, and the catcher would be just a shade out of position. Spahn stretched, took a quick look at Mays; Willie inched off first, nonchalant. As Spahn threw to the plate he took off for second. The pitch to Westrum was low and inside and the Braves catcher, off balance, threw late and badly to second. Willie had guessed right.

But he wasn't satisfied. Westrum was not a good hitter, and Maglie, the pitcher, was due up after that. It was time for bold action. On Spahn's next pitch to the plate Willie headed for third. Again the Boston catcher was caught off guard. His throw was far too late to catch Willie, who slid into the bag safely, stood up and dusted himself off, a wide grin on his face.

In the coaching box Durocher yelled at him, "You trying to give me heart failure, Willie?" But he, too, was grinning broadly.

The count now was three balls and two strikes to Westrum. Spahn came down with a fast ball, and the Giant catcher hit a fly ball to center field—an easy out, but deep enough for Willie to score the game's first run after the catch. Maglie, working masterfully, didn't need more than that, although the Giants gave him two more for insurance as he shut out the Braves, 3–0.

But in Philadelphia the Dodgers won, too, 5–0, and the race went to the last day of the season, still tied. If the season ended that way, there would be a three-game play-off series. The tension was electric. There hadn't been such an exciting pennant chase in years.

On the final day the Giants won again, behind Larry Jansen, 3–2, and the scoreboard at Braves Field showed the Phillies beating the Dodgers. In the Giant clubhouse the players sat undressed, or still in their sweat-stained uniforms, listening to the radio broadcast from Philadelphia. Dramatically, in the ninth inning the Dodgers tied the game. The Giants groaned. The game went into the tenth inning, the eleventh, the twelfth. Silently the Giant players urged on the Phillies. The pennant rode on every pitch, every play. Into the thirteenth went the game. At last, in the fourteenth inning the

Dodgers broke through and won the game. The pennant race had ended in a tie.

Suddenly it was as though the rest of the National League had vanished in smoke. New York City was the only arena and pitted in battle were the most colorful, traditional, bitter rivals in baseball history—the Giants and the Dodgers. The season up till then was written off; the home runs, the errors, the heroics and the mistakes were wiped clean. What had gone before counted for nothing. Only the Giants and the Dodgers remained and the best two out of three games would decide the pennant.

The city was charged with excitement. There had never been anything like it before. No World Series had ever engendered such enveloping interest. In the shops, in cars, in homes everywhere, all radios and television sets were tuned to the play-offs. People in the streets carried portable radios pressed to their ears, fearful lest they miss a single thrilling moment. The same question seemed to be on everyone's lips: "Hey, Mac, what's the score?"

On October 1st the play-off opened at Ebbets Field. Jim Hearn, who had won seventeen games during the regular season, started against Ralph Branca, and beat the youngster, 3–1, on homers by Irvin and Thomson. Giant fans held their breath. Were those the drums of victory they heard in the distance?

The Dodgers bounced back hard, however, demonstrating the power that had propelled them all season, beating the Giants, 10–0. The hopes of the Giant fans plummeted as rapidly as they had risen the day before. This, after all, was the true picture of the Dodgers. Weren't they the most powerful team in the league? Didn't they lead once by thirteen and a half games? It was miracle enough that the Giants had fought them to the wall; be satisfied with that.

Then the umpire called, "Play ball!" and it was Sal Maglie versus Don Newcombe, winner take all.

In the first inning the Dodgers got to Maglie for a run on walks to Reese and Snider and a single by Robinson. Sal got out of further trouble, but it was 1–0, Brooklyn. The score remained that way through six innings, as Newcombe mowed down the Giant hitters. Then, in the seventh, the Giants tied it, but the Dodgers rocked Maglie for three more in the eighth to take a 4–1 lead.

Defeated Giant fans headed for the exits. With Newcombe pitching brilliantly, it was all over but the formalities in the last half of the ninth inning. During the season's late drive the Giants had pulled off many a ninth inning rally. But now? How many miracles did anyone have a right to expect?

Al Dark led off for the Giants in the ninth. Newcombe got him to two strikes and a ball, then Dark singled to right. Don Mueller followed with another single and Dark sped to third. The exciting crowd hesitated. Dodger fans, gloating in anticipation of victory, stirred restlessly. Giant fans refused to hope. Monte Irvin stepped up to hit, fouled Newcombe's first pitch behind first. Hodges angled over, grabbed it for the first out. The exodus continued.

Whitey Lockman came up to the plate, and the next moment the stands were in an uproar as he doubled to left, scoring Dark and sending Mueller to third. The score now was 4–2, and the tying runs were in scoring position with one out. Time out was called. Mueller had twisted his ankle sliding into third, and Clint Hartung was sent in as a pinch runner. On the Dodger bench manager Charley Dressen made a decision—a decision that was to haunt him forever. He removed Newcombe and called in Ralph Branca to pitch to the next batter, Bobby Thomson.

As Branca took his warmup pitches on the mound, it seemed the entire city came to a standstill. Everything waited for the climax of this baseball drama. Finally the young right-hander indicated he was ready. Thomson dug in at the plate. The Polo Grounds grew quiet. Branca took the sign from catcher Roy Campanella, stretched, looked back at the runners, pitched a strike to Thomson. A great sigh seemed to escape from the huge crowd.

Branca stretched again, stopped, threw. Thomson swung. The ball leaped sharply from his bat and sailed toward left field. Andy Pafko raced back toward the wall. The crowd hung breathlessly for a moment—then burst into a roar as the ball soared into the left field stands for a home run. In the flash of a split second, defeat had become victory. The Giants had won the pennant!

A mighty swelling of sound seemed to rise from the city. Cries of astonishment, of joy, were heard wherever the game was being listened to or watched. As Thomson loped around the bases behind Hartung and Lockman, horns blew and whistles shrilled. Giant fans shouted to each other in the streets. In the Polo Grounds torn programs danced in the air like confetti. Hardened sports writers cheered and shook hands all around.

The Giant players were beyond celebration. They hardly knew how to show their delight. They pummeled each other and Thomson until every back was sore; Durocher and Stanky wrestled like children along the third base line. Willie Mays, wild eyed with joy, leaped around from man to man, shaking hands, hugging teammates, shouting aimlessly, "Say-hey! Say-hey!" till his throat burned with hoarseness.

After the incredible drama and heroics of the 1951 season, the World Series was expected to be an anticlimax. The New York Yankees, seeking their third straight World Championship, were rated far below the great Yankee teams of old, yet good enough to beat the Giants, worn out from their tension-filled battle for the pennant. In the words of one New York sports writer, it shaped up as a battle between "tradition, on the Yankee side, and momentum, on the Giants' side."

The Bronx Bombers won their American League pennant

with only one player hitting three hundred, rookie Gil Mc-Dougald, and Yogi Berra, who won the league's Most Valuable Player Award, batting in only eighty-eight runs. As with the Giants, the Yankees had a highly touted rookie outfielder, Mickey Mantle, who stacked up well against Willie Mays. Mantle played right field, alongside Joe DiMaggio in his last World Series. Hank Bauer and Gene Woodling were alternates in left field. At first base the Yankees had Joe Collins, at second Jerry Coleman, at shortstop Phil Rizzuto, and McDougald played third. Berra caught a mound staff that included Allie Reynolds, Eddie Lopat, Vic Raschi, Bob Kuzava, Johnny Sain and Bob Hogue.

The Giants' pitching staff did not measure well against this array. After Larry Jansen and Sal Maglie, each twenty-three game winners, there was little mound strength to be had. And both these hurlers were weary and sore armed from their regular season labors. Dave Koslo, Jim Hearn, Sheldon Jones, Norm Corwin and George Spencer comprised the bulk of the staff behind them. In the outfield the picture was brighter. With Willie Mays were Hank Thompson and Monte Irvin, Don Mueller having been hurt in the final playoff against the Dodgers. Whitey Lockman was at first, Eddie Stanky at second, Al Dark at shortstop and play-off hero Bobby Thomson at third. Westrum, Sal Yvars and Ray Noble did the catching.

When the Series opened at Yankee Stadium the day after the final play-off game, Leo Durocher, daring and desperate, threw in a surprise. Against Yankee ace Allie Reynolds he started left-hander Dave Koslo, who had compiled a mediocre 10–9 record during the season. Leo was counting on the momentum of the play-off victory to carry the Giants through the Series opener; furthermore, he needed at least another day's rest before starting one of his own aces, Jansen or Maglie.

72

Reynolds got past the first two Giant hitters in the first inning, then Thompson walked and Irvin followed with a single. Lockman doubled to score Thomson and send Irvin to third. A moment later Irvin electrified the fans with a steal of home, the first in a World Series since 1928. Thomson flied out, but it was 2–0, Giants.

The Yankees got one of the runs back in the second inning on a double by McDougald and a single by Coleman. It kept the game close until the sixth when Dark homered with Westrum and Stanky on base to break open the game. Koslo, pitching superbly the rest of the way, paid off his manager's gamble with a seven-hit five-to-one victory, the first time the Yankees had been beaten in a World Series opener since Carl Hubbell did it in 1936.

Willie Mays, playing in his first Series game, went hitless in five trips to the plate. He had hoped for better, of course, but by this time he was prepared for unassuming debuts.

Ed Lopat drew the Yankees even in the second contest with a three-to-one victory. The Series scene shifted to the Polo Grounds for the third game, with Jim Hearn facing Raschi. A standing-room-only crowd of 52,035 jammed the National League park, whistling and cheering as the Giants took their pregame batting and infield practice. Above the general din occasionally there could be heard the shrill cry. "We want Willie!" and manager Durocher, grinning, patted his protégé on the back warmly. "You're back home again, Willie boy. Those are your fans yelling for you out there. They're with you a hundred per cent, just like me and the rest of the team. Let's give 'em a little treat today, whatta you say?"

Willie nodded soberly. "I'll sure do my best, Mr. Leo."

He got his chance early. Raschi retired the first five batters to face him when, with two out in the second inning, Bobby Thomson hit him for a double. Up to the plate stepped

Willie, and the fans began a chant as they saw the colorful rookie up at bat for his first World Series in the Polo Grounds. "We want a hit! We want a hit. Let's go, Willie!" The chant became a roar as Willie responded by cracking Raschi's first pitch on a line over second base for a single. Thomson scored to put the Giants ahead, and Willie stood perched on first base, grinning broadly. It was his first World Series hit.

The score remained 1–0 until the Giants drove Raschi from the box in the fifth inning. Eddie Stanky opened the inning with a walk, and on Raschi's first pitch to Dark, Eddie attempted to steal second. Berra's throw to Rizzuto got there in plenty of time, but Stanky kicked the ball out of the shortstop's hand and went on to third before the startled Rizzuto could recover. Dark and Thomson each singled, Irvin was safe on a fielder's choice and Dark scored when Yogi Berra dropped a throw to the plate; Lockman applied the *coup de grâce* with a three-run home run.

After Thomson made out, Willie singled for his second hit of the game, but Bob Hogue relieved Raschi and put down the rally. The final score: Giants six, Yankees two, and once again the Giants led in the Series.

It rained the next day and as the experts liked to point out later, it served to cool off the hot Giants and give the Yankees time to reassemble their forces. Maglie faced Reynolds in that fourth game.

Willie was feeling fine after his two hits and a run batted in of the third game. In the second inning, with the score tied, 1–1, and Thomson on first base, he smashed a low line drive that exploded right at Rizzuto's feet—an extremely difficult ball to handle and one that almost invariably goes for a hit. Phil dug the ball out of the dirt and fired to McDougald to start a double play. In the fifth inning, with the Giants trailing 4–1, and two men on base, Willie came up again. This time he smacked a line drive off Reynolds' glove. Rizzuto, darting in from shortstop and seeing that there was no chance to get Willie at first, grabbed the ball and flipped to second for a force play on Thomson, robbing Willie of his second straight hit.

"You're hitting into tough breaks," manager Durocher said to Mays on the bench later.

Willie shook his head ruefully. "What does a man have to do to get a ball past that Rizzuto?"

Leo laughed shortly. "It's no shame to be robbed by Rizzuto, Willie. Keep swinging. You'll get through."

In the eighth inning with the Giants trailing 6–1, Willie had another chance to launch a rally. As he came up to bat, Irvin and Thomson were on base with one out. Willie took a ball and a strike from Reynolds, then rapped the next pitch right back past the mound. It bounded swiftly out toward center field, but Rizzuto, a blur of speed, cut off the hard bounder right behind second and, on the run, threw to McDougald to start another double play. Thus, in their three meetings, Rizzuto took three hits away from Mays. With them he took the game away from the Giants, and perhaps the World Series, too. The Yankees followed this win by taking the next two straight over the Giants, 13–1 and 4–3, for their third straight World Championship.

Willie added two more singles to his total in the final game, giving him four hits in twenty-two at-bats. In the six games he handled sixteen chances in the field without fault, and when it was over, Yankee manager Casey Stengel said of him, "That fella plays like he's been doin' it all his life, instead of being in the majors less than a year. He's gonna be great, that fella, you wait and see."

It appeared that the National League sports writers thought similarly. Afterward they named Willie "Rookie of the Year." It pleased him equally when at the same time

75

they named his manager and friend, Leo Durocher,"Manager of the Year."

On a barnstorming tour with Roy Campanella's All-Stars when the selections were announced, Willie made it a point to call Durocher at home. "We a good team, Mr. Leo," he chuckled over the phone.

"Willie," Durocher said, "you ain't seen nothin' yet."

THE SUDDEN LURCHING OF THE TRAIN AS IT SWAYED INTO THE railroad yards woke Willie from his fitful dozing. He yawned, stretched his cramped limbs and squinted out the window. Rows of freight cars were standing like patient cattle, and long chimneys like the guns on a battleship spewed dirty smoke into the air, making the sky gray, coating the window sills of his car with gritty soot.

Birmingham. Willie was home again, far from the cheers of the Polo Grounds and the happy weeks of barnstorming with Roy Campanella's All-Stars.

He swung off the train and looked around hesitantly. Someone called, "Willie! Oh, Willie!" He turned, his face brightening at the familiar voice. "Aunt Sarah!" he cried, and laughed as she rushed up to him, hugged him. Then she stepped back and surveyed him at arm's length. "I see you ain't missed your Aunt Sarah's cookin' much," she said. "Look at you, boy! Near fat as a brood sow!"

Willie guffawed. "That's muscle, Aunt Sarah!"

She snorted, poking a finger at his stomach. "They treatin' you good in New York?"

"I ain't complaining none." He looked past her. "Where's Pop?"

Aunt Sarah giggled. "Got him watchin' the ham in the oven. Joe Walker—you remember him—drove me down here. He's waitin' outside in the car."

They walked through the station to the street, and after Willie stowed his suitcases in the trunk of the old Ford they drove off through Birmingham, passing the mills and the shacks at the end of town, until they came to Fairfield. Near Aunt Sarah's house Willie said, "How's Mom?"

"I went by there just the other day," Mr. Walker said. "They all fine, Willie."

Aunt Sarah nodded. "Course, it ain't easy, Willie, what with your stepfather being out of work so much. They sure appreciate the money you been sending them."

"I want to take care of them the best I can," Willie said. "Just 'cause I been the lucky one, that's no reason they gotta be down."

Aunt Sarah kissed his cheek. "You're a good boy, Willie."

Mr. Walker pulled to the curb at Aunt Sarah's house, got out of the car and helped Willie with his bags. "Anything you need, Willie," he said, shaking his hand, "you don't forget to call me, hear?"

Later, alone with his father and Aunt Sarah, Willie relaxed in the familiar living room. Mr. Mays lit a cigar and squinted through the smoke. "How long you stayin' in town, Willie?"

Willie shrugged. "There's another tour coming up soon with Mr. Campanella. But depends on the draft board, I guess. I got to report in Birmingham in a couple of weeks. They gonna tell me how long I'll be in town."

Aunt Sarah looked up from her sewing. "Didn't you explain to them about how you support your brothers and sisters?"

He nodded. "Look like it don't make much difference, Aunt Sarah. And I tell you the truth, I don't want to make no fuss about it. Don't seem right, somehow. There's other

78

boys going into the Army all the time, guess I should go, too."

She looked at him shyly. "Bet that Mr. Durocher's gonna miss you plenty. I read in the Birmingham paper that you and him get on real good."

Willie looked surprised. "Didn't think the Birmingham papers knew anything about what's going on in New York." Then he sighed. "He's a fine man, Mr. Leo. Mighty fine. Yeah, I think that's one man who is gonna miss me. And I'm gonna miss him, too."

It took many months for the draft to call Willie, however. The red tape of office procedure and the question of the dependency of his mother and brothers and sisters kept the issue in doubt. Meanwhile he was content to forego further barnstorming tours for the familiar comforts of Fairfield. He visited his high school coach Jim McWilliams, and kept himself limber working out with the Fairfield Industrial School's basketball team, much to the youngsters' delight. Often he dropped by his mother's house, spending many hours with her and his half brothers and sisters. Soon, too, new furniture appeared in several Fairfield homes; a new couch and a television set for his mother, and food in the pantry to last them all many months; television sets for his father and Aunt Sarah, and a new rocking chair for Aunt Sarah.

In February, with his draft call still in doubt, the Giants called him to spring training in Phoenix, Arizona. It was time again for good-byes to his family, with friend Joe Walker standing patiently by the Ford, waiting to drive him to the railroad station. Once more, gazing out the window of the train, Willie was treated to the dismal parade of freight cars and factory buildings. Through the long hours of the ride to Phoenix he felt suffocated by an unaccountable gloom.

Leo Durocher was the first to greet him in camp. "What's with the draft?" he asked worriedly.

Willie shrugged. "Seems like they can't make up their minds."

"Let's hope they never do," Durocher grunted. "You in shape?"

Willie flexed his biceps. "Muscles like iron," he said.

Durocher felt them dubiously. "Yah, like my grandmother's," he snorted.

Willie broke into laughter. And suddenly the gloom lifted from his shoulders. He noticed how bright the Arizona sun shone, and the smile on his manager's face. He grabbed his glove and raced to the outfield. "Mr. Leo, you a card!" he shouted over his shoulder.

The Giants had every reason to be optimistic as the 1952 training season began. Statisticians had pointed out that the Giants, in sixth place when Willie joined them the previous year, went on to win eighty-one games and lose only forty with him in the line-up, a pennant-winning pace in any league. Now, here was Mays available from the beginning of the season. But Willie hardly had slipped into uniform when word came from his draft board that he was to be inducted into the Army at the end of May. Of the groans heard in Phoenix, Leo Durocher's was loudest of them all.

"Only one month!" he groaned. "We'll have Willie only for one month!" Then he set his lips grimly. "We've got to build up a lead in the one month to last us for the rest of the season without him!"

Further misfortune dogged the Giants, however. Two weeks before opening day, in an exhibition game against the Cleveland Indians, Monte Irvin broke his ankle. When the first ball of the regular season was thrown out, the Giants' optimism had worn a little thin.

Still, there was Mays, at least temporarily. On the third day of the season he robbed the Dodgers' Bobby Morgan of an extra base hit with bases loaded, by making a miraculous catch in deep left center field, then homered himself in the eighth inning of the same game to win it for Sal Maglie. With Willie patrolling the outfield like two men, hitting—not often, but when it counted—clowning in the clubhouse, providing the spark, the Giants were off and running, taking the lead in the National League race.

Willie's second home run of the season beat the Reds, 6–4. His third came the day after and beat the Reds again, 4–3, in the tenth inning.

His fourth was sandwiched between two doubles and beat the Dodgers, 3–0.

Then came the night of May 28th—Willie's final game before leaving for the Army.

A standing room crowd of more than forty thousand jammed Ebbets Field in Brooklyn, the largest crowd of the season anywhere in the league. It was "Farewell to Willie Night" in New York City. On the Dodger bench, the players were talking to a sports writer. "I suppose it sounds heartless," said Carl Furillo, "but as a Dodger I have to say I'm glad Willie's going."

"Me, too," said Pee Wee Reese.

"The man's a menace," Furillo went on. "I still haven't recovered from the way he threw out Billy Cox at the plate last year. I still refuse to believe it's possible, even if I saw him do it all over again. I've made some pretty good throws in my time, but there never was one like Willie's. Yes, sir, I'm not unhappy about his departure."

Jackie Robinson laughed. "That Willie, he's a pistol. Last night he doubled off the right field wall, homered over the right field wall, then doubled again off the right field wall. After the second double I walked over to him at second base.

"What's the matter with you, Willie?' I asked.

" 'What do you mean? Nothing's wrong with me,' he said.

" 'You're supposed to be a power hitter,' I told him. 'We shift toward left field on you and you slice the ball to right. It's not fair.'

"Willie scratched his head. 'Excuse me,' he said, 'I didn't realize it, Mr. Robinson.' "

Pee Wee Reese chuckled. "Yeah, that Willie's a hot one, all right. He's going to be a great ballplayer someday, too. With him gone the pennant race is a mighty different story."

On the Giant bench Leo Durocher sat with his head in his hands. "We're gonna miss him," he said to Arch Murray of the New York *Post*. "We'll miss him on the field and in the dugout. In the hotels and on the trains. We're going to miss his spirit and his unfailing cheerfulness. We became a better ball club from the minute he joined us and it wasn't all because of his bat and his arm and those great plays he made in center field. He kept the club spirit alive. The locker room won't be the same without him."

"You really think that much of him," Murray said.

"He's the only kid I know who has a chance to be another Joe DiMaggio, the greatest I ever saw. Just think. Willie's only twenty-one, with less than ten months of organized ball behind him. He's just learning how to hit, to understand how the pitchers have been fooling him. Why wouldn't we miss him?"

Willie didn't get a hit on his farewell night, but the Giants won, 6–2, giving them a lead of two and a half games over the second place Dodgers. In the locker room after the game, the usual horseplay was forgotten. The players gathered around Willie, shaking his hand in farewell, and Bill Rigney gave him the team's good-by gift—a portable radio.

Willie was overcome with gratitude, not at their gift, but at the token of their affection for him. He choked up, fumbled for words; then, blinking through the blur of his tears, he raised his fist above his head.

"Just hold 'em till I get back, boys!" he cried.

Everyone laughed and patted him on the back. Manager Durocher, standing in the background, turned to broadcaster Dizzy Dean, the once great pitcher for the St. Louis

Cardinals. "See what I mean, Diz?" Durocher said. "The Giants without Willie would be like our old Gas House Gang without Pepper Martin. He's the heart and soul of this ball club."

Later, after most of the players had dressed and left, Leo and Dean drove Willie to his hotel in upper Manhattan. There, while Dean waited in the car, Leo walked through the lobby to the elevators with Willie. At the doors he gripped Willie's hand, opened his lips as if to speak, then closed them silently, shook his head, sighed and walked away.

A week later the Giants tumbled to second place. They remained there for the rest of the season.

Willie spent two years in the Army, serving as a physical education instructor at Fort Eustis, Virginia. He had ample opportunity to play ball with the Fort Eustis baseball team, and while competition in the Army was largely unprofessional, on opposing camp teams he met such pitchers as Vernon Law of the Pittsburgh Pirates and Johnny Antonelli, the Boston Braves pitcher. On occasion, when the Army granted him a weekend pass, Willie headed directly for wherever the Giants were playing, anxious to lend moral support, fidgeting on the bench as his teammates played through a losing game. There were many such losses in 1953, and they dropped to fifth place in the final standings.

Willie's own playing was severely curtailed in 1953. During the summer his mother died, and he went sorrowfully back to Fairfield for the funeral. The Army granted him a two-week leave, and it was several weeks after that before he felt like playing ball again. Then, back in action in August, he chipped an ankle sliding into second. Fortunately it wasn't a serious break, but he was in a cast for six weeks. Until he tested the foot again and found it fit, the Giants—from owner Horace Stoneham down to the bat boy—were a nervous crew indeed.

Considering the sad state of the Giant fortunes from the day Willie left them in 1952, it was small wonder that they were overjoyed when he rejoined them in March of 1954. Right after his discharge from the Army, Willie flew directly to Phoenix to join them in spring training. They were in uniform and on the field when he arrived by taxi from the airport. Except for clubhouse man Eddie Logan the locker room was empty. Willie began stripping off his clothes even before he said hello.

Logan ran over and pumped his hand. Then he said, "Hey, you getting into uniform, Willie? You just got out of the Army. You just got off the plane."

Willie waved him aside impatiently. "Where's my locker, that's all I want to know."

Logan still couldn't believe him. "You really gonna play today?"

Willie looked at him. "There's a game today, ain't there?"

"Sure, they're playing one right now."

"Then I'm getting dressed." He reached into the locker Logan indicated, put a Giant cap on his head.

Tom Sheehan, chief scout for the team, walked into the room, saw Willie, hurried over to shake hands. "C'mon, Willie, what's taking you so long!" he grinned.

"Hey, Tom," Willie laughed, "my cap don't fit."

Logan grinned at him. "Maybe your head got too big reading the papers, Willie."

Willie threw the cap at him playfully. "You know I never read no papers." He looked around the room. "Say-hey! Where's Mr. Leo?"

"On the field," Sheehan said. "Waiting for you like an expectant father."

Sal Maglie came through the doorway, dripping wet after pitching batting practice.

"Hey, Barber, where you been?" Willie called to him.

Maglie looked up, grinned. "In the shower."

Willie laughed. "Hey, ain't that where I left you?"

Coach Freddie Fitzsimmons entered the locker room next. "Hey, Freddie, I want to hit!" Willie yelled, dressing all the while.

"Too late, Willie," the coach said. "We got new rules here. A player comes to work late, he don't get a chance to hit."

"I'm hurrying, I'm hurrying," Willie said in mock despair. "Please let me hit, Freddie."

By now word had spread that Mays had arrived. Photographers and reporters pressed into the locker room. Flash bulbs popped; a chorus of questions was hurled at Willie. Chub Feeney, the Giants' vice president, elbowed his way through. "Let him out, let him out," he said to the newspapermen. "The season'll be over before he gets out there."

Finally the picture taking and questioning were over, and Willie ran through the alleyway leading to the dugout, carrying his glove and a bat. A murmur of recognition spread through the crowd in the stands as he emerged; it grew into a roar of excitement as the fans saw Durocher leap off the bench, throw himself at Willie and grasp him in a headlock.

"Mr. Leo! Mr. Leo!" Willie cried, gasping and laughing. "Hey! What you doin' to me! Lemme loose! Lemme on that field!"

Durocher wrestled with him a moment longer, then pushed him onto the bench, sitting down beside him. Reporters gathered around. Willie had eyes only for the action on the field. "You gonna let me play today, Mr. Leo?" he asked.

"What about it, Leo," a writer asked. "You letting Willie play, fresh off the plane and out of the Army?"

Durocher laughed. "Just off the plane and out of the Army, huh? Listen, if this was opening day instead of spring training and he'd just stepped off the plane I'd still let him play."

The intrasquad game was in its fifth inning. Durocher waved Willie in to pinch hit against rookie Pete Modica. He took two balls and a strike, then slammed the next pitch far over the left field wall, more than four hundred feet away. Swiftly he circled the bases, trotted to the dugout and sat down again next to Durocher.

"You see that, Mr. Leo? You see how I hit that ball?" he said excitedly.

Durocher looked at him calmly. "Against a rookie pitcher? My grandmother coulda done it."

Willie clutched at his sides in laughter. "Mr. Leo, you the funniest man I ever met!"

For the first time in nearly two years, Durocher felt an inner peace. Willie was back.

8

THE FLAGS FLEW BRAVELY OVER THE POLO GROUNDS ON APRIL 13, 1954. The huge crowd was in a holiday mood. It was opening day of the season, the Dodgers against the Giants, and there in the batting cage, banging baseballs into the left field seats, was Number 24—Willie Mays. For Giant fans once again, the slogan was "All's right with the world."

There were plenty of skeptics around the major leagues, despite the terrific .381 pace of Willie's spring training hitting and the many examples of his fielding acrobatics. There were some who thought Willie would be lucky to hit .250 for the regular season. Privately, the Giants hoped he could hit .275 and bat in seventy-five runs. "If he can do it," one Giant executive confided to a reporter, "we have a good chance to take the pennant."

Surprises were in store all the way around in 1954.

The groundskeepers at last began to clear the infield, and the fans clapped in rhythm impatiently, waiting for the game to begin. Then Sal Maglie ambled to the mound, took his final warmups, the national anthem was played and the plate umpire shouted, "Play ball!"

Maglie and his opponent Carl Erskine pitched through the

first inning flawlessly. In the second Roy Campanella homered for Brooklyn; in the third Al Dark homered for the Giants with one man on base; in the fourth Campanella homered again; in the fifth Henry Thompson homered to make the score 3–2, Giants, but the Dodgers tied the score on three hits in the sixth.

In the home half of the sixth Willie was first man at bat. Erskine, working grimly, threw two strikes past him, then wasted a pitch for a ball. Sweating profusely with the pressure of the duel, Erskine came back with a fast curve. Willie swung, connected, and the ball sailed deep into the left field seats for a home run. Final score: Giants four, Dodgers three, and the fans gave Willie a standing ovation as he gathered in Carl Furillo's fly ball for the last out of the game and trotted off the field.

In the clubhouse Durocher was exultant. "Hey, what I tell ya," he repeated as visitors streamed into the locker room, "we got a winner, we got a winner!"

But the opening day's victory had its deceptions. On paper the Giants did not look like the strongest team in the league, and few sports observers predicted much improvement over their fifth place finish of 1953, even with the return of Willie Mays. The team lined up with Whitey Lockman at first base, Davey Williams at second, Alvin Dark at shortstop and Henry Thompson at third; the outfield had Willie in center flanked by Don Mueller in right and Monte Irvin in left. Wes Westrum was the catcher; pitchers were Sal Maglie, Johnny Antonelli, Hoyt Wilhelm, Don Liddle, Marv Grissom, Ruben Gomez and Jim Hearn. In the latter department the Giants were considered woefully deficient.

Following the opening day victory, the pattern seemed to follow preseason predictions. By the first week in May, though Willie had won four games singlehandedly with home runs, the Giants were in fifth place. And Willie himself, despite his game-winning homers, was batting in streaks, hot and cold, with an average hovering at .250. Durocher was far from satisfied. The team was in Pittsburgh, on the last leg of its first road trip, when he called Willie aside in the clubhouse and asked to see him in the manager's office.

Willie followed Leo, his face deeply troubled. Durocher sat down in a swivel chair behind the desk; Willie remained standing, clutching his cap. "Mr. Leo," he said, before Durocher could begin talking, "don't holler at me. I'm no good if you holler at me."

Durocher sighed. "I'm not gonna holler at you, Willie," he said quietly. "But you ain't been doing right."

Willie lowered his eyes. "I know, Mr. Leo. They been gettin' me out. But I don't know what I'm doin' wrong."

Durocher got up, walked around the desk and assumed a batting stance at Willie's side. "Here's how you've been holding your feet, Willie," he said. "You expect to get into the Hall of Fame standing like that in the batter's box? You look like a mother hen setting on an egg."

Willie laughed.

Durocher shifted his feet. "Here's the way you should be standing. See my feet?" Willie nodded. Durocher went on. "Another thing, you've been hitting everything to left field. A guy like you, with your power, you should be slicing homers to right. Heck, Willie, you're the greatest!"

Willie looked down at the floor, abashed. "I'll remember what you say, Mr. Leo." He hesitated, then, "Show me once more about how I should hold my feet."

Durocher showed him. That afternoon Willie beat the Pirates, 2–1, with a home run and a game-winning double in the ninth inning—into right field. Three days later, in the Polo Grounds, a home run and two doubles beat the Braves, 6–3; the next day a triple and two singles drove in four runs in a 7–4 win over the Braves. By the end of May Willie was hitting over .300 and the Giants were in second place, hot on the trail of the Dodgers.

Still there were skeptics, waiting for the bubble to burst. But the Giants rolled on, spurred by Willie's hitting and fielding. There was an occasional falter, but Leo Durocher was there in an instant, teasing, praising Willie into regaining stride. "You're the greatest, Willie, how come you messed up a play like that?" he might say. Or, after a particularly exciting catch by Willie, "Humph, my grandmother could of done it—and she's over eighty." Willie delighted in Leo's deprecations, bursting into loud laughter at each one.

In June the Giants caught the Dodgers, passed them and opened up a four-game lead. And one by one, the skeptics faded away. Even when the Giants lost, Willie looked spectacular. There was a game in June against the Braves, for example, at the Polo Grounds. On the first pitch of the game Bill Bruton hit a terrific drive to dead center field. At the crack of the bat Willie turned and began to run. The ball was hit so high and far that, as Willie ran, Chub Feeney and Tom Sheehan, Giant executives sitting at an office window above the center field clubhouse, had time to make a bet. "Willie'll never make this one," said Sheehan. "Betcha a cigar he does," challenged Feeney. Then they kept their eyes on Willie.

Willie kept running. His cap flew off as he ran. First he looked over his left shoulder, checking the flight of the ball; then he looked over his right shoulder, all the while running at full speed. Finally he was running on the gravel at the far reaches of the outfield. Once more he looked over his shoulder, then, his back still to the plate, he looked upward, extended his hands full length, caught the ball on the dead run and almost slammed full force into the clubhouse —-more than four hundred and fifty feet from home plate.

The crowd went wild. It was one of the greatest catches ever seen in baseball. Silently, Tom Sheehan handed Chub Feeney a cigar. "I saw it," he said, "but I still don't believe it."

An inning later Willie homered, to give the Giants a 1–0 lead, but the Braves rallied later to win the game, 5–2. The following day, however, Willie made sure his batting efforts were not in vain. He waited until the ninth inning, with the Giants losing, 1–0, then hit a two-run homer to win it. The home run was his twenty-third of the season, giving him the league lead over Stan Musial.

The tenacious Brooklyn Dodgers were keeping pace, however. Led by the slugging of Duke Snider, Jackie Robinson, Carl Furillo and Gil Hodges they tied the Giants for the lead late in June. Manager Durocher prowled the dugout. "Hang in there, men, hang in there," he urged. "Let's win 'em one at a time."

It was the evening of June 25th at the Polo Grounds. The scoreboard showed that the Dodgers had won their afternoon game, taking a half game lead. On the pitcher's mound for the Giants was Ruben Gomez, opposing Bob Rush of the Chicago Cubs. For four innings the two men fought a scoreless duel. Then, in the fifth, Randy Jackson of the Cubs hit a two-run homer to give the Chicagoans the lead. The Giants got one run back in the sixth, but into the last of the ninth the score remained Cubs two, Giants one—and the grim reminder of the Dodgers' afternoon victory stared the Giants in the face on the scoreboard.

Lockman led off in the ninth and Rush got him on a ground ball to the second baseman. Dark singled, but Mueller popped out. Up to the plate stepped Willie. He dug in and Rush went to work. The Cubs pitcher stretched, took a look over his shoulder at Dark, pitched to the plate. Willie swung and missed. The crowd groaned. "C'mon, Willie!" a fan shrieked, "belt one!" Another leaped to his feet, brandished his fist. "Say-hey! Let's show 'em, Willie!"

Willie stepped out, rubbed dirt on his palms and stepped back in. Rush stretched, threw. Willie swung; there was a sharp crack and center fielder Frankie Baumholtz turned

91

around and began running. The ball was hit far over his head, near the edge of the cinder path in deep center field. By the time Baumholtz caught up with the ball, Dark was heading toward the plate with the tying run and Willie was rounding second, racing for third. As Dark crossed the plate, Baumholtz's throw started for the infield—and Willie kept on running, right around third for home.

The fans leaped up screaming, exhorting Willie onward. Willie thundered for the plate, his cap flying off. Down the line he came as the throw-in flew to catcher Walker Cooper. Ball, Willie and Cooper came together in a cloud of dust as Willie slid in. Umpire Dusty Boggess peered into the dust cloud. "Safe!" he bawled.

In the third base coaching box Leo Durocher leaped into the air. The Giants had won, 3–2, remaining tied for first place with the Dodgers.

That was the season's turning point. After the Cubs left the Polo Grounds, the Giants took two straight from the Cardinals, Willie winning the second game in the tenth inning when he doubled, stole third and scored on Henry Thompson's fly ball. Then the Dodgers came in for a three-game series. Three in a row the Giants beat them. The final game was an 11–2 rout, led by rampaging Willie, who drove in five runs with two homers, his twenty-ninth and thirtieth of the season.

The Dodgers left the Polo Grounds four games behind; they never recovered from the three-day beating.

The Giants, and especially Willie Mays, were riding high. Every day was celebration day in the clubhouse. If they won, they felt they would never lose another; if they lost—so what? They would win tomorrow was the feeling. Laughter and high spirited horseplay filled the locker room. Willie's "Say-hey's" boomed and echoed off the lockers and through the hissing of the showers. It looked as though the growing bubble would never burst. The All-Star game arrived in mid-July and Willie and Duke Snider were named to share center field for the National League. Only twenty-three years old, Mays was the youngest man on the field that day.

In the midst of all this glory, personal tragedy again caught up with Willie. In Cincinnati, shortly after the All-Star contest, a phone call from Fairfield informed him that his beloved Aunt Sarah had died.

At once Willie flew to Alabama. Before he left he went to his manager and told him, "I know how much you need me, Mr. Leo. I don't mean it bragging like—you know how I mean it—but Aunt Sarah—I just got to go there, Mr. Leo."

Durocher put his arm around Willie's shoulders. "I'd be mad at you if you did anything else. Of course you got to go. I want you to go. You take off and don't worry about a thing. Skip the next couple of games. Meet us in Milwaukee Friday, how's that?"

Willie blinked through his tears. "I'll do that, Mr. Leo. You're a good man."

Durocher was embarrassed. "Aah, so's your grandmother," he said.

Willie tried to smile. Then he turned away and was gone.

In Fairfield hundreds turned out for Aunt Sarah's funeral; she was long known, respected and loved in the town. Willie spent two days there, mostly sitting in silence in the old living room, remembering the long years that had somehow raced by unnoticed, recalling the happy days he had spent in that simple, love-filled home as a child. Now his mother was gone; Aunt Sarah was gone. Toward dusk of his second day in Fairfield Willie rose from Aunt Sarah's old rocking chair, silently packed his bags and took a cab to the airport.

In the clubhouse at Milwaukee's County Stadium his teammates greeted his return warmly. "Say-hey!" his roommate Monte Irvin mimicked him, "We missed you, kid!" Maglie walked over and shook his hand. "Glad to see you back, Willie." Dark, Westrum, Thompson, Lockman, An-

93

tonelli and the rest stopped by to tell him how sorry they were at his loss, but how happy they were to see him back.

Willie dressed quietly, and one by one the players got into uniform and went out on the playing field. Willie was last. He walked through the tunnel leading to the dugout, came out into the night air, crisp and clean. The field was ablaze with light for the night game. The breeze whipped the flags atop the grandstand. Some of the fans spotted him and began to applaud; the applause was taken up and spread throughout the stands. Durocher came over to him, shook his hand. "Glad to have you home," he said.

Willie took a deep breath. Yes, he thought, this was home. Not the steel mills and the gray shacks of Fairfield. There was nothing for him there any more. Memories, perhaps, and his father and his brothers and sisters, whom he loved dearly. But it wasn't the same. Home was here, where the air smelled clean and the grass was emerald green under the bright lights; where he heard the warm laughter of his teammates, who were also his friends, and the sharp crack of the bat hitting the ball. Home was the smell of leather and liniment in the locker room, and Mr. Leo slapping at him in the shower with a wet towel. Home was the good feeling when you made a tough catch, when you got good wood on a ball and zoomed around the bases while fans cheered you. Home was baseball. Home was the Giants.

That night against the Braves he beat Warren Spahn in the ninth inning with his thirty-fourth home run of the year. By the time the Giants' road trip ended five days later, he had hit his thirty-fifth and thirty-sixth.

He returned to New York a conquering hero. He had become the idol of the city, and of Giant fans in particular. With his outfield spectaculars, his grinning boyishness, his new-found homer-hitting prowess, Willie had captured the imagination of millions of hard-boiled New Yorkers. Not since the heyday of Mel Ott had Coogan's Bluff honored a

Giant player to such an extent, taken him so completely to heart.

Willie was the subject of dozens of interviews, newspaper and magazine stories. His picture was featured on the covers of such non-sports magazines as *Look* and *Time*. He appeared on TV shows such as "What's My Line" and Ed Sullivan's "Toast of the Town." A song was written about him, called, "Say, Hey, Willie," and on a Saturday night TV variety show he appeared on stage while behind him a chorus sang and danced to the tune. He was besieged with offers to do advertising testimonials, front for fund-raising organizations, work for automobile agencies, insurance companies, politicians and what have you. By the dozens they clamored to see Willie, some with legitimate offers, some seeking dishonestly to capitalize on his tremendous popularity.

He basked innocently in the limelight, often wondering what the fuss was all about. But the Giants were anxious about him; not for fear the adulation would turn his head—they knew Willie better—but that in his innocence he might be taken advantage of. Therefore they assigned to him Frank Forbes, a former prize fight judge and professional athlete, whose job would be to advise and guide Willie in his personal affairs.

Forbes sought out the young hero in the clubhouse one morning and talked to him privately. "Willie," he said, "first thing I want you to do is tell me everything you do or want to do—off the field. There's nothing you're going to do, or want to do, that I haven't done and maybe suffered from or benefited from. You're famous. You're going to get a lot more famous. You're going to meet a lot of people. They'll tell you nice things. It'll cost you something. You talk to me first—it'll be my pleasure. Maybe it's not nice to say, Willie, but from now on every smile, every handshake, you've got to evaluate it. Because eighty per cent of the time it's because you're Willie Mays of the Giants and they're looking to separate you from your money."

Forbes talked on for a while, watching Willie's reactions to his lecture, sizing him up, weighing the youngster's questions as he went along. Finally he straightened up and said, "Okay, Willie, I guess that about sums it up. Now, is there anything you want?"

Willie grinned. "Yeah. I'd like to buy a big white Cadillac."

Forbes's jaw dropped, then he burst into laughter. He turned away, shaking his head, and staggered into manager Durocher's office. "Hey, Leo," he said, jerking his thumb over his shoulder, "is that kid for real?"

Durocher looked up. "What kid?"

"Mays. Willie. The Say-Hey Kid."

Durocher grinned. "He's for real, all right. Why?"

Forbes scratched his head, then his face turned sober. "It's hard to believe, that's all. He's really a kid, a babe in the woods. He don't know the score yet, does he?"

Durocher shook his head. "And it'll be a sad day for him when he learns it."

Forbes nodded. "I know what you mean. It's fantastic, to meet a kid who's getting the publicity and the adulation he's getting, and still find him so decent, so naïve. At first I thought he was putting on an act."

Durocher laughed shortly. "It's no act. Willie's heart is as naked as the day he was born. He doesn't know any other way to live."

Forbes sighed. "I hope I'm up to the job of keeping him that way."

"Try hard," Durocher said. "For the kid's sake, Frank."

Forbes nodded, then left to begin his job as Willie's guardian angel.

Fortunately, help appeared several days later. One morning, as Willie lay in bed reading one of his favorites, a mystery novel, a rapping came at his door. At his summons, in came Joe Walker, a friend of the family from Fairfield.

Willie sprang from his bed, pumped the other man's hand. "Joe, what brought you to New York?"

Walker looked around at the room. "What kinda place is this you're living in, Willie?" he asked, ignoring the greeting.

Willie was taken aback a moment. Then he said, "They call it an apartment hotel, or something like that. Nice, ain't it?"

Walker sniffed. "Ten o'clock, and you still in bed?"

Willie pouted. "I don't have to be at the park before eleven, and I'm always the first one there. It ain't far from here."

Walker snorted. "Had your breakfast yet?"

Willie was eager to please, and he began to sense the note of criticism in Walker's tone. "Not yet, Joe. Wait just a few minutes. I was just gonna hop into the shower and get dressed. Then we'll go downstairs and I'll buy you a whompin' breakfast."

Walker nodded sourly. "Downstairs, eh?" He sat down on the rumpled bedclothes and looked about him with distaste. In a few moments Willie rushed out of the shower, threw on underclothes, slacks and a sports shirt and whisked Walker out into the street. There he guided him into a corner luncheonette, chose a booth near the rear, ordered juice, ham and eggs, toast and coffee for both of them.

"Now," Willie said, "you still haven't told me what you're doing up here in New York."

Walker leaned back as the waitress brought the food, then motioned silently for Willie to begin eating. He waited until they were drinking their coffee before he spoke. He was an older man, with the beginnings of gray at his close-cropped sideburns, and he spoke with a quiet dignity.

"Willie," he began, "I was a good friend of your mother and your Aunt Sarah for a long time. I remember you when

97

you was crawlin' bare in your mother's house, when your grandfather was alive and prayin' you wouldn't wind up in the mills. Now they all gone. Before your Aunt Sarah died, she called me to her house and she told me what she wanted me to do. 'Joe,' she said to me, 'I want you to go to New York when I'm gone, and see after my boy Willie. He's the kind of boy needs regular folks. Those ballplayers, they're always travelin' around,' she said, 'eatin' in restaurants, livin' in hotels, takin' up with all kinds of people.'

"'Willie, he ain't used to that kind of livin',' she said. 'He likes his eggs done so, and his ham just right, and he likes to have a person around to talk to. So you go to New York, Joe, and you fix Willie up right. It's been botherin' me for a long time, wonderin' about how he's livin' up there,' she said to me. 'Will you do it, Joe,' she asked me, 'so's I can close my eyes knowin' my Willie's bein' looked after?'"

Willie looked down at his coffee. "That's what my Aunt Sarah said?"

Walker nodded. "And now you know what I'm doin' here."

Willie rocked back and forth for a moment, a look of deep sorrow on his young face. Then he sighed deeply. "I ain't doing nothing wrong, Joe," he said. "But I got the feeling you don't like the way I'm living anyway."

"It don't mean nothin', what I like or don't like," Walker replied. "It's what your Aunt Sarah would like."

"What should I do?"

Walker started to speak, hesitated. "Uh, could I order some more coffee, Willie?"

Willie smiled and motioned to the waitress to refill their cups. "Piece of cake, Joe?"

"No, no," Walker waved his hand. "Coffee's just fine." He sipped at the cup when it was brought, then cleared his throat. "Before I came to see you I went scoutin' around up in Harlem. I got a few old friends up there who come from

98

'bama. They steered me onto a perfect place for you to live, Willie. It's with a nice woman name of Goosby. Anna Goosby. She's a fine lady who's gonna remind you just of your Aunt Sarah. Cooks like a queen. Southern style."

Willie looked interested. "Where is this place?"

"St. Nicholas Place. Wanna go up now?"

"Well, does this Mrs. Goosby know about me? I mean, about you wanting me to live in her place?"

"Sure. And she's thrilled about the idea, Willie. Why, you'd be like a grandson to her."

Willie looked uncertain. "You don't think she'd mind havin' me around, cooking for me?"

"I told you," Walker explained patiently, "I already spoke to her about you stayin' there. She said it was just the thing you needed, havin' a place like a regular home. And she'd be happy to cook for somebody and have a person to talk to."

Willie nodded. "Let's go." He paid the check, returned to his hotel, paid his bill, packed his suitcases and moved in that day with Mrs. Goosby. Walker returned to Fairfield, his mission accomplished.

It was the final days of July, and with his thirty-six home runs Willie was ahead of the pace set by Babe Ruth the year he established the major league record of sixty home runs. Day by day the count was kept: Willie was two days ahead of Ruth's pace; he was three; he was one; he was five. Naturally the sports writers asked him how he felt about threatening Ruth's mark.

"I don't even want to think about it," he said. "All I do is go up and swing where the ball is pitched. The minute you start thinkin' about hittin' homers you stop gettin' them."

Nevertheless, Willie hit them with astounding regularity in July, until finally the opposing pitchers began throwing to the outside of the plate, away from his power. Willie began slicing pop flies to the outfield for easy outs, but with his batting average hovering at the .320 mark, nobody was worrying.

Nobody, that is, except Leo Durocher.

There was a night game against the Pirates in the Polo Grounds. As usual during these halcyon days the locker room was bubbling with good humor. Manager Durocher wandered around casually, smilingly, clapping a back here, rubbing a head there. On a stool in front of his locker Willie was lacing on his spikes. Durocher walked by, clapped him on the shoulder and said quietly, "Finish lacing your shoes, Willie, then meet me over at the Coke machine."

Willie's fingers fumbled hurriedly with the laces. Finished, he got up, walked deliberately indifferent to the machine, pulled out a soft drink, and jerked off the cap. Leaning against the machine was Durocher, sipping at a bottle. "Willie," he said between sips, as casually as though he were discussing the relative merits of their soft drinks, "I want you to stop hitting home runs."

Willie almost gagged on his drink. "Wh-what you mean, Mr. Leo?"

"I got a new strategy," Durocher whispered. "I've been working it out. Most of the time you hit homers, there's nobody on base, right? I mean, that's the percentage, because then the pitchers ease up on you a little more. So I figure we're better off if you just get on base, so that Thompson, Irvin and Rhodes, who've been hitting homers pretty good lately, can knock you around the bases. And at the same time, Willie, you'll be getting more hits, and I got a hunch you can win the batting championship this year if you try."

The theory had more holes in it than Swiss cheese, Durocher knew, but the purpose was to keep Willie from concentrating on hitting homers. Durocher knew, too, that Willie would believe it even if he told him the best thing for the Giants was that he sit on top of the flagpole in center field. There was more to solving the problem than merely stating his so-called "theory," however, and Leo hoped that at this point Willie would help by asking the right question. Happily, Willie did.

"But Mr. Leo," he said, "you know I just hit the ball where they pitch it. If I ain't trying to hit homers on purpose, how can I stop?"

Durocher breathed easier. He had the answer ready, the answer he felt would make Willie the most dangerous hitter in the league. "Shift your feet, Willie, like this," he said, and demonstrated, gripping the pop bottle like a baseball bat. "This way you'll be spraying line drives to center and right, instead of poling high flies to left. Get it?"

Willie nodded eagerly. "Say-hey, that's a good one!" He chuckled. "Gonna be a lot of fooled pitchers around this league before long."

Under his breath Durocher muttered to himself. "I wonder how much dough a psychologist makes a year?"

9

VERNON LAW, PITCHER FOR THE PITTSBURGH PIRATES, MOPPED his brow with the sleeve of his sweat shirt and looked out at the scoreboard, checking the ball-strike count. Two balls, two strikes on the batter Willie Mays. He checked the Giant runner leading off second, Al Dark. It was a tough spot, and the sweat poured from him, though the night air was cool. The score was 1–1 here in the bottom of the ninth inning, and there was Mays, waving his bat menacingly with the winning run on second base. Willie already had jolted him for a double and a single and had scored the lone Giant run. This despite the fact that Law had been curving him over the outside corner of the plate all night. The pitcher was puzzled; the last time he had faced the Giants he had gotten Willie out four times in a row the same way. Law couldn't know, of course, about Leo Durocher's little lecture to Willie a few hours earlier.

Now he stepped back on the mound, stretched, checked Dark, threw to the plate. It was a curve that broke over the outside corner. Willie leaned into the pitch and lined it into right center field for a hit; running all the way, Dark scored easily with the winning tally.

Except perhaps for Law, no one in the league was surprised at Willie's performance that evening. But as the days passed and Willie, though continuing to hit, failed to connect for even one homer, speculation arose that either he was ill and losing his strength or the pitchers were wise to him and denying him home runs. The pitchers, as a matter of fact, could have testified to the truth—Willie had wised up to them; his average slowly and steadily was moving upward.

His popularity did not wane with the slowing-up in his home run production. In the midst of the summer's adulation, Hulan Jack, Manhattan borough president, proclaimed August eighth Willie Mays Day, the supreme honor given by a city to one of its ballplayers. During pregame ceremonies at home plate, sign-bearing youngsters sang the Willie Mays song, and he was given dozens of presents from his teammates, the fans, and even the Polo Grounds ushers. Finally, he was given a plaque by the Catholic Youth Organization as the most popular player in New York.

Willie was too overcome with emotion to say much. He smiled, waved to the cheering crowd, shuffled his feet, said a brief, "Thank you, thank you all very much," and proceeded to show his appreciation by banging two doubles and a single during the game for a 6–3 Giant victory.

Early in August the rest of the team was not faring as well, however. They bogged down in a prolonged slump, were playing less than .500 ball while the Dodgers crept to within two games of them. Aided by teammate Don Mueller, Willie kept them on top. He hit in twenty-one straight games, raising his batting average to .340 and during all that streak he hit but one home run—an amazing tribute to his ability to follow his manager's directions.

Willie was supremely happy. Adored, feted, publicized, playing at the peak of form, he was the picture of contentment. He acted like a tonic on the rest of the players. As the late season jitters struck the team his overflowing good humor kept them on an even keel. "How can you be in the dumps with a guy like Willie around?" Whitey Lockman remarked to a reporter one day. "We blow a game and sit around all gloomy in the clubhouse, and there comes Willie out of the shower, grinning with all his teeth. 'Say-hey, tomorrow's another day!' he yells, and somehow, well, a lot of that tension seems to just melt away."

Monte Irvin, Willie's road game roommate, was especially benefited by his light heart. Irvin was a room pacer, a chronic fretter who tortured himself often with self-recrimination. Like a caged lion he would roam their hotel room, pounding the wall with his fists in frustration after a bad day. "How can you sit there like that!" he cried one night to Willie, who was sitting calmly propped up in bed, munching an apple and reading a western. "Don't you realize we're in trouble, the Dodgers are catching up? We're slumping for weeks now!"

Willie looked up from his book, surprised at the outburst. Then he shrugged. "Tomorrow gonna come, Monte, no matter what I do today." And he went back to his book.

For a moment Irvin stared at him, shifting between anger and disbelief. Looking at Willie curiously, he weighed his roommate's words. Then he chuckled to himself. After a while he got up, undressed and crawled into bed. In minutes he was fast asleep.

When the Giants were at home there was nothing Willie could want. Or almost nothing. Often Irvin, who lived in New Jersey, would come by Mrs. Goosby's place in the morning and pick Willie up in his car. It was then that Willie would feel the one pang of want. As he climbed in beside his friend he would run his hand wistfully over the new leather upholstery of the convertible. "Wish that Mr. Forbes would let me get that white Cadillac," he would say. And then it was Irvin's turn to laugh.

Otherwise Mrs. Goosby's was Aunt Sarah's all over again.

Willie had a quiet, airy, spick-and-span room in her home. She kept unnecessary callers from bothering him, fixed him his ham and eggs and hash brown potatoes for breakfast, talked with him when he wanted to talk, let him alone when he preferred it that way. He was content to sit for hours alone in his room, listening to records on the phonograph his teammates had given him on his Day.

When the Giants played a day game Willie was always the first to dress and leave the clubhouse, much to the consternation of Leo Durocher, who liked it when Willie hung around joking with him and the other players. He wondered for weeks where Willie was rushing off to, until late one afternoon he decided to drive up to Mrs. Goosby's and investigate.

Durocher left the Polo Grounds, drove swiftly to Harlem, turned down 151st Street to St. Nicholas Place. As he turned the corner he nearly ran over a sport-shirted figure dashing madly for a manhole cover that was marked out as second base. Braking his car to a stop, Leo leaned out the window. "What's the matter with you, you nuts?" he barked at the man in the sports shirt.

Willie walked over to the car. "Why am I nuts, Mr. Leo?" he inquired mildly. "It ain't dark out yet."

That's the way it was with Willie. If the sun was still shining, then a man should be playing ball, even if it was a stickball game with a bunch of youngsters on a Harlem street. As Durocher sat there gaping, his car was surrounded by a dozen or more clamoring kids. "Hey, you're not gonna take Willie away, are you?" one of them shouted. "We need him for the game!"

Willie grinned. "I'm a four-sewer man, Mr. Leo," he said. "That's pretty good hittin' in this league. Like hittin' it into the bleachers in the Polo Grounds."

Durocher leaned back against the seat. What could you say to a boy like Willie? Don't play stickball with these kids in the street, it doesn't look right for a major league ballplayer? No, you couldn't say that, not to a boy like Willie. Maybe, Durocher thought, sitting there, maybe it's because Willie belongs there in that stickball game, belongs to those worshiping kids, as much as he belongs to the Polo Grounds. More, maybe.

So he simply grinned as he said to Willie, "Don't forget what I told you, watch out for those outside pitches," and gunned the car down the street. Willie watched it for a moment, then turned back to the game. "Say-hey," he called, "who's up? C'mon, I'm on second base and Mrs. Goosby's gonna call me up for supper any minute. Let's get goin'."

As the pennant race went into its final month, interest in the league centered on the battle between the Dodgers and Giants for the flag, and on the battle for the batting crown among Willie, teammate Don Mueller and Duke Snider of the Dodgers. Down the stretch the two teams and the three players fought: the Giants' lead see-sawing—two games in front, then three, then four, then plummeting to two as they dropped a doubleheader; and the players—first Snider on top with .342, trailed by Willie and Mueller, but the three of them so close that each hit scrambled their positions.

On September 13th, with two weeks left to the season, Willie doubled against the Cardinals, setting up the run that won the game, 1–0. It was his eighty-second extra base hit of the year, breaking Mel Ott's all-time Giant record. Then came the showdown series with the Dodgers, the final week of the season. The Dodgers had to sweep all three games to stay in contention; the Giants were determined to clinch the pennant with the first game. Sal Maglie faced the Dodgers' Don Newcombe.

Big Don, having a mediocre year, started off badly. After retiring Lockman he walked Dark and Mueller singled. In stepped Willie. Newcombe, working him carefully, got behind, three balls and a strike. He came in with the next pitch, a good curve over the outside—but a little too good.

Willie leaned into it, lining the ball into right center field. Dark trotted home, Mueller spun around the bases and scored the second run as Willie pulled into a second with a double.

Working masterfully, Maglie kept the Dodgers in check until the fifth, when a home run by Jackie Robinson made the score 2–1. But in the Giants' sixth Willie took over again. With Mueller on third and two out he singled, to make the score 3–1. Thompson followed with another single, Irvin cracked a home run, and with the Giants' lead now 6–1, the pennant was just about wrapped up. In the ninth Willie singled again, came around to score the final run. The score: Giants seven, Dodgers one. The Giants had won the pennant.

There was nothing left now but the batting race. Willie's three hits in the pennant clincher gave him a four-point lead over Snider and five over Mueller. But on the final day of the season the three men were so close that it required the carrying of their averages out to the fourth decimal place to separate them. Mueller was leading with an average of .3426, followed by Snider with .3425 and Willie with .3422. The way the schedule had worked out, Snider was favored to retain his lead through the final game, because while he and the Dodgers were facing Jake Thies of the Pirates, Willie and Mueller were up against the Phillies' Robin Roberts, one of the game's greatest pitchers and the strike-out leader in 1954.

Thies held Snider without a hit. Mueller got a hit his first time up; Willie followed with a hit. That made the order Mueller, Willie, Snider. Both Mueller and Willie failed their next trips. Mueller failed again on his third, but Willie tripled. Mueller failed again on his fourth try and Willie doubled. He had the lead now, with one more at-bat to go. Roberts walked him, while Mueller made out—and Willie was the batting champion of the National League.

The final batting figures were: Willie, .345, Mueller, .342,

Snider, .341. Willie also hit a total of forty-one home runs, which meant that from the day in late July when he had been told by Durocher to stop going for homers, he hit only five, a testimonial both to Willie's adaptability and Durocher's teaching. Besides winning the batting crown, Willie led the league in triples with 13, was third in runs, scored with 119, tied for third in homers and his hits totaled 195. He also set a new all-time Giant mark for extra base hits in a season with eighty-seven.

Winning the pennant was one thing—beating the Cleveland Indians in the World Series would be another. With a record-breaking 111 victories, the Indians had vanquished the Yankees to take the American League pennant. They had a superb pitching staff: Bob Lemon and Early Wynn had led the league, each with twenty-three victories; behind them were such stalwart moundsmen as Mike Garcia, Bob Feller and Art Houtteman. Cleveland also had power, personified by such hitters as Al Rosen, Larry Doby, Bobby Avila and Vic Wertz.

Despite their convincing performance during the season, the Giants were decided underdogs against the Indians.

Durocher sent his ace, Maglie, against Bob Lemon in the opener at the Polo Grounds. For seven innings the two pitching masters were locked in a 2–2 tie. Then, weakening, Maglie got in a jam in the eighth. Indians led off first and second with one out, and Vic Wertz was at the plate. The Cleveland slugger had already touched Maglie for three hits in the game. In the crisis, Durocher replaced Maglie with Don Liddle. The Polo Grounds was taut with excitement as Liddle took his warmups, then signaled that he was ready.

Wertz settled into position. Liddle stretched, checked the runners and threw a fast ball. Wertz swung—and slammed the ball high and deep to center field. The runners led off cautiously—the Indians had had occasion to see Willie's miracles in spring exhibitions—but this hit looked uncatchable. Still Willie kept running, his back to the plate. He ran, took a fast peek over his shoulder, put his head down and ran some more. Finally, more than 450 feet from home plate, running full speed toward the bleacher wall, he reached over his left shoulder and the ball dropped into his glove.

Willie wasted no time waiting for cheers. He braked hard, spun to his left, lost his cap, then heaved a mighty throw to the infield before the astonished runners could get back, tag up and take the extra base. Newspapermen, players and Cleveland manager Al Lopez all agreed that it was an impossible catch. One of the greatest ever seen.

It gave the Giants the reprieve they needed. Once again Willie had provided the impetus for his teammates. Durocher replaced pitcher Liddle with Marv Grisson, who finished up the inning. The game continued through the ninth and into the tenth innings. With one out in the Giant half of the tenth, Willie worked Lemon for a walk. On the first pitch he stole second. Since he represented the winning run, Lemon intentionally walked Thompson, setting up a possible double play. Durocher countered the strategy by sending up Dusty Rhodes, his phenomenal pinch hitter, for Irvin. Swinging on Lemon's first pitch, Rhodes popped a lazy fly ball down the right field line, but with the right field stands at the Polo Grounds only 260 feet from home plate at the foul line, the ball dropped into the stands for a home run.

The opening game of the Series went to the Giants, 5–2. There was some bitterness in the Cleveland press about the "cheapness" of the pop fly homer, but manager Durocher laughed it off. "Maybe it wasn't much of a hit," he admitted, "but still you had to have a ticket to catch it. Besides, you have to give us defensive credits. If it wasn't for Willie's catch there wouldn't even have been a tenth inning."

Having thus gotten off on the right foot, the Giants completed their rout of the Indians, much to the surprise of practically all baseball experts. They won the next three straight to become World Champions, the first time in forty years that a National League team had won a Series in four straight games.

Willie wound up with a .286 average, driving in three runs, scoring fours others and collecting four walks in the four games. It was conceded everywhere in baseball that 1954—his first full year with the Giants—was one of the greatest years ever experienced by a young player like Mays. With the World Series tucked away in the records, the post-season honors began to fall upon him. The Baseball Writers Association of America named him the Most Valuable Player in the National League. *The Sporting News,* baseball's official trade publication, named him Player of the Year in his league. The Associated Press poll of national sports writers and sportscasters named him Male Athlete of the Year. The New York baseball writers, in their separate annual voting, gave him the Sid Mercer Award. He was given the $10,000 diamond-studded Hickok Belt as the Professional Athlete of the Year. In addition he was the recipient of the annual B'nai B'rith sports award and a host of other honors awarded by private organizations.

When it was all over, and the awards received and tucked away, Willie was happy, somewhat bewildered by the frenetic pace of the award dinners, and very tired. At his side during the rush of luncheons and banquets in his honor was adviser Frank Forbes. The two men were sitting one evening in Mrs. Goosby's place, the furor having died down, and Forbes said to him, "Well, Willie, I guess you won just about everything but Horace Stoneham's teeth. And now I've got a present for you, too. Now I'm going to let you buy that white Cadillac you always wanted."

Willie grinned at him. "That's the best news yet, Mr. Forbes," he said. "But you know somethin'? I changed my mind. Instead I'm gonna get a yellow Lincoln with a black top. Ain't that gonna be the greatest?"

10

WILLIE COULDN'T SIT AROUND IDLE FOR LONG. SOON HE TIRED of going to the movies and playing stickball in the streets; he needed sterner competition. So with teammate Ruben Gomez he got permission from the Giants to play winter ball in the Caribbean League, joining the Santurce, Puerto Rico, team. As usual when he broke into a new league, Willie started miserably. He didn't get a hit in his first twelve trips to the plate, and the Caribbean crowds began to wonder what the fuss was about Willie Mays—until he broke out of his slump, got eleven hits in his next thirteen tries and wound up the Caribbean season with a .395 average.

In mid-January Horace Stoneham, Giant president, flew down to Santurce to check on Willie and Gomez and, while there, to sign them to 1955 contracts. And there was a further reason. Willie and Ruben had been involved in a fist fight that had made sports headlines back in New York, and Stoneham wanted to smooth any hard feelings remaining between his two stars. The argument had been a silly one, involving whose turn it was at batting practice, and it was written off as a bit of nervous tension after the heat of the pennant race and World Series a few months before. As a matter of fact, by the time Stoneham arrived, the two men had shaken hands and called off the feud.

There was little left for the Giant president to do, there-fore, but sign them to contracts. After watching the Santurce team beat a Cuban rival behind Gomez's pitching and Willie's hitting, Stoneham walked into the clubhouse, took over the manager's office and, after Willie and Gomez had dressed, asked them to step in, one at a time, and chat. Gomez was first—and easy to sign. Then in came Willie. After the usual preliminary amenities, Stoneham came to the point. He drew out a contract, pointed to the salary figure already filled in, and looked up at Willie. "Okay with you, Willie?" he asked, smiling. "A nice fat raise over last year."

Willie looked at the figures for a moment. "I don't know, Mr. Stoneham, I got to check with the boss first."

Stoneham nodded, then did a quick double take. "What do you mean, check with the boss? I'm the boss. I own the Giants, remember?"

Willie nodded his head. "Yes, sir, Mr. Stoneham. But I mean Mr. Leo. He's my boss."

Stoneham began to laugh, then he saw that Willie was serious. He shrugged, picked up the phone and called Durocher long distance at his home in California. He spoke to his manager briefly, then put Willie on. Willie listened a moment, told Leo what the contract called for. He turned to Stoneham. "Mr. Leo say I should ask for five thousand dollars more."

Stoneham's jaw dropped. "What! Why, that—" Then the ridiculous humor of the situation got to him, and he burst out laughing. "Okay, okay, Willie, you got it. Now hang up before Leo makes me give you a piece of the Polo Grounds." He rewrote the salary figures on the contract, giving Willie a new one for thirty thousand dollars, almost twice his salary of the year before. Suddenly, Willie was up among the high-salaried ballplayers.

Stoneham flew back to New York after that, but Willie and Gomez stayed on, playing into the month of February as Santurce competed in the Caribbean World Series. By the time they reported for spring training in March, the two players were beginning to feel the strain of so much baseball. This was especially true of Willie, who had to play every day, while Gomez, as a pitcher, had to work only every fourth or fifth. He didn't complain of his weariness at Phoenix, where the Giants were in training, but it showed through, and occasionally he mentioned it.

He came out of the shower one afternoon after a practice game, sat down on a stool in front of his locker, his face troubled. Durocher, standing near the rubbing table, talking to trainer Doc Bowman, looked over at him. "Hey, what's eating you, Willie?" he called. "Don't tell me you're still sore about the umpiring down in Puerto Rico?"

Willie laughed. "No, though man, they sure were blind, some of those guys."

"Then what is it?"

"I want to buy a house."

"A house?" echoed Durocher. "What are you gonna do with a house?" Suddenly his eyes narrowed. "Hey, you got a girl?"

Willie changed the subject abruptly. "No, nothing like that, Mr. Leo," he said, which was untrue, since he had met a girl in New York in whom he was seriously interested. But it was true that it wasn't the problem on his mind at the moment. "I guess I don't really mean I want a house," he said. "All I want is a bed. Man, I'm so tired. All I know is I'm never gonna play down in Puerto Rico no more."

"What are you kicking about?" Durocher laughed. "You've got a soft touch for the next six weeks. Nothing to do but play a few innings in the exhibition games and be ready opening day."

"Oh, I'll play, Mr. Leo," Willie said quickly. "Don't you

113

worry about me. I'll play nine. But like I say, I ain't goin' down to the Caribbean no more. Man, I'm beat."

Durocher laughed, as did other Giant players in the clubhouse. Whatever Willie said seemed to get laughs; by now it was tradition. Willie himself laughed, but inside he felt the weariness of the long months of uninterrupted baseball, banquets, interviews, popping flash bulbs, handshakes and speeches.

It didn't show up in spring training, mostly because Durocher took him out of the exhibition games in the early innings. In fact, Willie was sensational in training, poling homers in quick succession all over the spring "grapefruit" circuit. Playing in Los Angeles against the Indians one day, he put on a show neither the Angelenos nor the Indians would forget for a long time. In batting practice he hit sixteen pitches over the fence, five of them in a row, then just to prove he could do it in competition, in the game he doubled off Bob Feller, following that with a homer off Don Mossi and another off Ray Narleski before Durocher took him out for a rest.

But when the regular season began, his skills began to betray him. The instincts he had always relied on became his enemies, forcing him into lapses at the plate and in the field. It happened suddenly; so suddenly and so completely that it was hard to believe this was Willie Mays, who had been compared to Musial, Cobb, Speaker and DiMaggio combined into one.

Playing against the Dodgers in the first week of the season, he let himself be picked off third in the seventh inning of a 1–1 ball game that eventually was won by the Dodgers. Two days later, against the Phillies, he neglected to touch second base on a hit and was tagged out. He began throwing to the wrong base on hits to the outfield. Fly balls that would have been routine for him in the past dropped in for extra base hits. Then one day, making an easy catch on a fly ball in his

114

unusual basket style, the ball popped out of his glove and went for a two-base error. The fans at the Polo Grounds booed him.

In the locker room later, questioned about the use of his basket technique on fly balls, for the first time in his major league career Willie lost his temper. "All right," he screamed at the sports writers, "make a big story out of it! Go ahead! But I'm gonna go on catching 'em like I always have and no fans' booing is gonna make no difference." He paused then and added, a little sadly, "I never heard nobody booing me before."

The sports writers filled their columns with speculation. What was wrong with Willie? Too much winter baseball, too many testimonial dinners? Had fame turned his head? Was he feeling the responsibility for carrying the team? Whatever it was, Willie was having a bad time of it. He was hurt, confused, harried by the pressure of his failing talents. Yet the harder he tried to work his way out, the worse he looked. Even his attempts at the old Willie Mays humor seemed to fall flat, or worse, go astray. On the Giant bus taking the team to Crosley Field in Cincinnati one day, he started to grapple with pitcher Marv Grissom. It had always been good for a laugh, but this time Grissom hit his head against a light bulb, shattered it and had to be taken to a hospital to have his scalp sewn.

Durocher was at a loss for a solution. How to account for such a complete reversal of form? Not that Willie was doing that badly, on paper. He was hitting .270, had seventeen homers and forty-two runs batted in by mid-June, but the figures were deceptive. He was barely a shadow of the Willie Mays who led the team to the 1954 World Championship. And with him suffered the Giants, of course. They were floundering in fifth place, far behind the league-leading Dodgers. Durocher knew he must try something.

"Willie," he said one day, "I think if your hitting straightened out, the rest of your troubles would, too. And you know, you're doing wrong what you did wrong early last season. You're pulling the ball to left field too much. You're hitting into too many double plays on hard-hit grounders. Remember what I showed you last year?" He went into a batting stance, showing Willie the position of his feet. "Start hitting to right again, Willie, and you'll be okay."

But this time Willie seemed to pay no heed to his manager's advice. Three days later, with the situation unchanged, the Giants pulled into Milwaukee. During batting practice before the first game, Durocher, as was his custom, posted the day's batting order on the wall of the dugout. Playing center field was not Willie, but young Gail Harris. Nobody noticed it at first, since most players glanced cursorily at the list as they passed, checking their own position in the line-up. And who would have dreamed that Willie Mays would ever be benched?

Hardly Willie himself. He trotted off the field after chasing fungoes for a few minutes, heading for the water cooler. He glanced at the line-up, took a drink, then looked again. He pressed his face up close, ran his finger up and down the list several times to make sure. His name was not there. For a second he panicked; then he chuckled to himself. That Mr. Leo, playing jokes on me to cheer me up, he thought. Well, he would go along with the gag.

Willie sought out the Giant coaches, Freddie Fitzsimmons, Frank Shellenback and Herman Franks. To each one he put the same question. "Hey, what's the matter? How come Mr. Leo don't have me in the line-up today?"

But as each coach shrugged and finally one said, "Don't ask me, ask Leo," Willie lost some of his assurance. Maybe it wasn't just a joke?

He went to Durocher. "Mr. Leo, how come my name ain't down for the game today?"

Durocher avoided looking at him, staring out to the field instead. "Look, Willie, the way you're hitting, my grand-

116

mother could do better. We're losing with you, so we can lose without you. Maybe you're tired. Maybe you need a rest."

"Oh, no, Mr. Leo, I'm not tired!" Willie protested.

"Well, sit down today anyway. Watch how some of the other guys hit the ball to right field."

Willie patrolled the dugout that afternoon like a restless tiger. He couldn't sit or stand still. He jumped up from the bench; he sat down again; and he wore a path to the water cooler. The Giants won, 5–3.

The next day Willie's name again was missing from the line-up. He approached Durocher before the game. "Mr. Leo, can't I—"

"Don't need you. Doin' okay without you."

Almost in tears, Willie turned away.

On the third day Durocher put him back. There were no miracles. Willie did not begin hitting and fielding in his accustomed style right away. But there was improvement. With grim determination showing on his features, he played a tighter game; his throws no longer went astray; his fielding, while not spectacular in the old sense, was adequate enough —no pop flies fell in for base hits. At the plate he began picking up a few points here, a few points there. The home runs continued to drop in regularly, and in addition there was a sprinkling of singles and doubles to right and center field.

As the Giants came off their western swing they stopped in Minneapolis for an exhibition game. Willie got only one hit, a right field double, but afterward Durocher said to him, "Now why can't you swing like that all the time? You looked so easy and relaxed, like a completely different player."

Willie stared at him. "I didn't know I was doing anything different, Mr. Leo. What was I doing?"

"Forget I even said anything," Durocher said hurriedly. "I don't want you to think about it. That way maybe you'll do it."

Willie went hitless against the Cardinals next day, but Durocher was still satisfied with his swing. The day after that he picked up three singles and two walks in a double-header. Then it was back to New York for three games against the Dodgers. In the first he banged four singles, in the second a double and two singles. But it was in the final game of the series that Willie served notice that he was back in form. He hit two home runs and a single to drive in all the Giant runs in a 6–1 victory.

The clubhouse rang with some of the old cheer. Willie was approaching the .300 mark and with him, the Giants, as the season neared its mid-point, moved out of the second division and into a battle for third place. Still, these weren't the Giants of 1954. Something was missing. Antonelli wasn't pitching well, nor was Gomez. Sal Maglie, who had toiled so long and faithfully, was feeling the effects of age and injuries; he was sold to the Cleveland Indians at the end of July. The late inning rallies that keynoted the Giants' championship team the year before were not forthcoming this time. Durocher wheedled, cajoled, barked, but it was all the team could do to remain in the first division. There were even rumors that some of the players were beginning to resent the way their manager was treating Willie—giving him the big smile and the pat on the back while at the same time growling at them.

Durocher's explanation that Willie was that kind of personality sufficed when he was a rookie, and when the team was going well. But when the situation deteriorated, and the club began to flounder, hidden resentments sprang up, new ones came forth as in their anger, their frustration at losing, some of the men sought a scapegoat. In his innocence, Willie was oblivious to it all.

As the season drew into September it was apparent that nobody, least of all the Giants, was going to catch the Dodgers. But down to the wire Willie played all out to win.

A week before the end, when it didn't mean much any more —except to Willie—he injured himself smashing into the Polo Grounds wall chasing a fly ball. An ambulance rushed him to the hospital, but except for a nasty bruise and a headache he was all right. His only regret was missing his final turn at bat. He had hit a single, a double and a triple in his first three tries, and with fifty homers for the year, he needed but one more to tie the Giant record held by Johnny Mize.

That record-tying homer eluded him until the last game of the season, when he hit one off Phillies' hurler Jack Meyer to win the finale, 4–2, securing the Giants' third place position. It was a far from satisfying season for Willie, though he finished with a .319 average, fifty-one homers, and thirteen triples, leading the league in both departments, and one hundred and twenty-seven runs batted in, second in the league only to Duke Snider, who had one hundred and thirty-six. The statistics were excellent, but Willie felt that with his early season slump he had let the team down.

Hardly had the last of the season been recorded when Willie received a bad shock; Leo Durocher announced his resignation as manager of the Giants. The new manager would be Bill Rigney. Willie could hardly believe it. "What am I gonna do without you, Mr. Leo?" he wailed. "Nobody but you can be my boss!"

Durocher comforted him. "It had to come sometime, Willie. You know baseball. Managers come and go. Rigney's a good man, you'll get along with him fine. I'm gonna be watching you all the time, and I expect you to give a hundred per cent for him same as you did for me."

"Oh, you know I'd do that all right, Mr. Leo," Willie sniffed. "But . . . but it ain't gonna be the same with you gone. No matter what."

"No, Willie," Durocher agreed. "It ain't gonna be the same. For me either."

11

THE GRAY RIBBON OF THE NEW JERSEY TURNPIKE FLASHED beneath the wheels of Willie Mays's cream convertible; he had bought a Cadillac after all, instead of a Lincoln. It was still dark, the chill dark of a February morning just before dawn. The radio was blaring forth jazz, and in their happiness Willie and the pretty girl beside him were oblivious to the needle of the speedometer. Suddenly Willie glanced into his rear view mirror, uttered, "Oh, oh!" and eased his foot off the gas pedal. He slowed down, turned onto the shoulder of the road and braked to a stop. Behind him a trooper's car pulled up, its roof signal blinking the red chase warning. The trooper got out of his car and approached Willie's.

"License and registration," he said automatically, hardly looking at the occupants of the car. Willie handed him both. The trooper examined them, looked up suddenly as he read the name on the certificates. "Hey, Willie Mays!"

Willie grinned at him. "That's who, officer."

"You know you've been speeding like you're chasing a fly ball or something," the trooper said. "What's the big hurry?"

"Well, officer, me and the lady here—this is Miss Marghurite Wendelle—we're goin' to Maryland to get married."

"No kidding! That's funny, didn't read anything in the papers about you getting married."

Willie nodded. "It was kind of a spur of the moment thing, you know? We been going together for more than a year, quiet like. And just last night we decided to head for Elkton and get married just as quiet."

The officer shook his head. "Well, I'm sure sorry I got to delay you, Willie, but you'll have to come to the station with me and pay your fine for speeding."

"Oh, don't worry about that, officer," Willie said. "I don't want no special favors. If I was speeding, I want to pay my fine. Teach me a lesson for next time."

He followed the trooper's car into the Ballmawr, New Jersey, station, paid a fifteen-dollar fine, and with the blessings of the local police force continued on his way to Maryland. There, in Elkton, he and his bride-to-be were joined by several friends at the Bethel African Methodist Episcopal Church for the ceremony. The reverend who was to officiate had no idea who the couple was. He glanced at the license, then took a second look at Willie. "Say, are you THE Willie Mays?"

Willie nodded, smiling.

"I enjoyed seeing you on television a number of times," the reverend said. "This certainly is a thrill, marrying you and this lovely lady here." Willie, still smiling, remained silent. The reverend cleared his throat and went on to the ceremony.

By the time Willie and his wife returned to New York, the word had gotten back, and they were mobbed by reporters and photographers. His marriage was a complete surprise, even to the Giants and Willie's personal adviser Frank Forbes. "I knew Willie had been seeing Marghurite," he said, "but I couldn't pin him down on anything definite."

Willie and his bride answered the barrage of questions good humoredly: where did they meet, where were they going to live, and so forth. Then a reporter asked, "Hey, how about a honeymoon, Willie? Where you going?"

Willie laughed. "Honeymoon? Man, I got to report for spring training in three days. This is the honeymoon!"

The newlyweds moved into a house Willie had bought on St. Nicholas Place, not far from Mrs. Goosby, so that his wife would have company during the long stretches when the Giants would be away. Three days after the wedding he reported to Phoenix, to prepare for the 1956 season.

He opened spring training like a whirlwind, better than he ever had before. Willie himself couldn't explain it. "I don't know," he remarked to Arch Murray of the New York *Post* one day, "I just feel so strong it scares me sometime." His expression came after he had hit a home run in Tucson that traveled so far out of the park it was lost to sight.

Murray mentioned Willie's optimism to manager Rigney, and the new Giant pilot agreed with the appraisal. "Sometimes he scares me, too," Rigney said. "I mean, he just looks too good to be true. You remember that homer he hit off Art Houtteman couple of days ago? I was watching the play closely. Houtteman fooled Willie on the pitch. He didn't get good wood on it at all. So the ball went maybe only four hundred feet out of the park."

Willie's pace through the spring exhibition schedule was devastating. With a week to go before the start of the season, he was hitting an astronomical .476, which included eleven homers and twenty-eight runs batted in. What was more, he was running the bases like a frightened deer. Stealing had never been a major part of Willie's repertoire, despite his great speed. In fact, it hadn't been until the season before that Durocher had let him run at all, and he had stolen twenty-four bases. Now, in the spring of 1956, Rigney had given him orders to run, to steal the umpires' teeth if he could, and in exhibitions Willie was showing he could do it.

He was secretly pleased that Rigney was letting him run.

He liked flying around the bases, taking risks, playing danger-ously, upsetting the opposing fielders. It was exciting base-ball. It was one of the things that he had most admired about Jackie Robinson, the way the Dodger star had run bases. Playing against him, Willie had watched Jackie carefully, tried to learn from him and emulate his base running style.

Now Rigney was giving him open orders to run pretty much as he saw the opportunity. He had been worried about that, worried that precisely because Durocher had started him running the year before, Rigney would put the reins on him.

He wondered how Rigney felt about him, wondered whether he had been one of the players who had resented his being Durocher's favorite. Willie was apprehensive. Would Rigney be deliberately tough to prove he would play no favorites? He sighed regretfully, thinking about it often that spring. Oh, how he would miss Mr. Leo! But there was nothing to do but wait and see what would happen, how he would make out with Rigney.

No matter what, Willie knew, his job would remain the same—to run and hit and catch. In the exhibition games to come, he meant to show his new boss exactly how well he could do all three.

In the final day of a series in New Mexico against the Orioles, Willie hit three home runs and a triple, and in the press box a veteran baseball observer remarked, "It's in-credible. He's the greatest hitter I've ever seen. I've been around since Ruth and Gehrig, and I've seen them all. I thought that Yankee kid Mickey Mantle was the greatest around today, but I've changed my mind. There's no telling where Mays can go. He can break every record in the book in his playing lifetime."

Then within ten days, Willie braked to a near standstill. He got three singles in his next twenty-two times up, and, remembering that Willie's early 1955 slump was blamed on too much training, Rigney sent him home to rest out the remaining exhibition games. "It's tough on the fans," the manager said. "But we open in four days and the important thing is to have Willie ready then."

The rest cure seemed to work. Willie began the season brilliantly, and the Giants were once again full of high hopes for the pennant. True, such stalwarts as Maglie and Irvin were gone—the Giants had traded Willie's old roommate at the end of the previous season—but there were new, young names on the roster that held promise. Foster Castleman, Daryl Spencer, Eddie Bressoud, Gail Harris, Bob Lennon and Allan Worthington were expected to back up Willie with their youth and spirit. Somehow, it went unnoticed that as the 1956 season opened, Willie himself was not quite twenty-five years old. And therein might have held the answer to the mystery of what befell the 1956 Giants.

On opening day Willie served notice on the league's catchers that this year he was their sworn enemy. His first time at bat against the Pirates he singled, stole second, stole third and scored on a fly ball. Then, with the score tied in the ninth, 3–3, he slammed a one-out double. Thompson, batting next, hit a slow ground ball to the shortstop, who fielded the ball routinely and threw to first, conceding third base to Willie. But Willie didn't stop at third. He never intended to stop at third. He just flew around the bag and thundered for home. The Pirates were caught so unawares that by the time they unraveled themselves and got the ball home Willie was in safely with a dust storm slide that won the game.

The Polo Grounds was thrown into an uproar. This was the old Willie Mays—with a new wrinkle added.

On the second day of the season Pirates pitcher Ronnie Kline held him hitless for eight innings. As the game went into the ninth, 4–4, Dark doubled with two out. In stepped Willie. Kline pitched him outside for a ball, over the inside corner for a strike, then again outside—and Willie rammed a single right through the middle to score Dark with the game winner.

It was quite a beginning. Fans were talking 1954 all over again, even when the Giants lost the next two in a row. Who could win 'em all? the fans shrugged. The important thing was that Willie was running wild again. Willie. Willie. That's all you heard when talk was about the Giants —Willie making his basket catches. Willie losing his cap. Willie said this and Willie said that. Willie hit a homer and Willie stole a base. Willie made another great catch. So Durocher was gone, so what? They said he was the genius who knew how to make Willie tick, and there'd be trouble with him gone. So now he's gone—and look at Willie play!

The Giants won one, then dropped two. C'mon, Willie! came the plaintive cries from the grandstand. Willie responded. Playing the Phillies, he singled in the first Giant run, then stole second and scored the second run. But in the eighth inning the Phillies led, 7–6. Lockman worked Murray Dickson for a walk. Dark singled and it was up to Willie again. Rigney, coaching in the third base box, called down to him. "Let's get ahold of one, Willie boy!"

Willie took a ball, a strike, then fouled off two pitches. The fans began a chant. They stamped their feet. Willie dug in. Dickson came down and Willie swung. The ball jumped off his bat. The Phillies left fielder took two steps backward, turned and stopped. The ball sailed high into the upper left field stands for a tremendous home run. Willie had won another one.

But as May began the Giants were in fourth place. There was Willie, and little else. Of the pitchers only Johnny Antonelli showed a consistent ability to win. Rigney juggled his line-up, trying various combinations, looking for the winning one, but the pieces didn't fit.

May sixth was Willie's twenty-fifth birthday, hardly a cause for celebration with the Giants now in sixth place.

But he lit his own candles, at the expense of Cardinals' catcher Bill Sarni. He walked his first time up and stole second on the first pitch, beating Sarni's throw easily. His second time up he singled. Sarni was watching him carefully this time, but Willie stole again and went to third when the hurrying catcher threw wildly to second base.

When Willie walked his third time up both Sarni and pitcher Vinegar Bend Mizell worked with one eye on him and one eye on the batter. But again Willie went down, and again he beat the throw. Only this time, after he had picked himself up out of the dirt, he proceeded to steal third on the next pitch and went all the way around when, beside himself with rage, Sarni threw the ball into left field.

With all of Willie's base stealing, the Cardinals still held a 4–3 lead going into the eighth inning. Up for the fourth time, Willie singled. Now Mizell and Sarni were going to hold him to first or nail him on a steal attempt if they had to pitch out to the batter four times. They tried it twice, but Willie just stood off first and grinned at them. They couldn't try it again, couldn't walk the next batter intentionally with the game so close. They watched Willie like a pair of buzzards eying a wounded jack rabbit. Mizell pitched to the plate—and Willie was off. Sarni grabbed the pitch and tore off his mask. He could see at once Willie had the base stolen, but he had to throw the ball, if nothing else than out of sheer frustration. He watched as Willie slid in safely, then threw his mitt to the ground and stomped over to the water cooler. At that moment he was ready to hand in his catching tools and take up another trade.

A moment later Willie scored the tying run on a single, and the Giants went on to win, 5–4.

It was shortly afterward that Willie went into a prolonged slump. It wasn't the usual kind of slump, where a batter finds himself going long stretches without a hit, when line drives get caught and the breaks seem against him. Rather it ap-

126

peared that Willie had lost something—faith perhaps, or hope, rather than his talents. He was playing drab ball, except for occasional flashes of brilliance, as though suddenly he would awaken from his lethargy and discover he was Willie Mays, and act accordingly. There was a game-winning homer here, a brilliant catch there, a rash of stolen bases, then nothing for a week. What was ailing him?

Among professional baseball observers there were two distinct schools of thought, plus a third that straddled the first two. Theory number one was that Willie Mays wasn't Willie Mays without Leo Durocher. He needed that warm relationship with his manager, needed the frequent pat on the back and the genial critique, the gag lines fed to him by Leo. It was these things, the theory went, that made life with the Giants so pleasurable to Willie. Only when it was a big happy game could he operate with complete relaxation, at top efficiency. All this was not meant as criticism of Bill Rigney, who could not have been a Leo Durocher any more than Durocher could have been a Mel Ott. The simple fact was that Rigney was friendly but not effusive, and he was determined from the first to treat no player with special favor. And, said this school of theorists, Willie was a player who needed that extra attention. Without it, he was the Willie Mays of 1956, rather than of 1954.

The second theory was the more cold-eyed one. It looked down the Giant line-ups of 1954 and compared them with those of 1956. In the year of the World Champion Giants Willie had hitters in front of him and hitters in back of him —Mueller and Dark in front of him, Thompson and Irvin in back of him. Enemy pitchers got a rough workout from the center of the batting order. They couldn't afford to concentrate on getting Willie out.

Now Mueller was held back with a leg injury and having a terrible year. So was Dark. Irvin had been traded and Thompson, beaned early in the season, hadn't yet recovered.

The rookies weren't coming through. Therefore, these theorists claimed, each time Willie went up to hit he felt the burden. It was all up to him. Go for the homer, because there's nobody behind you gonna hit you in. He pressed, tried too hard. It was, in fact, the reason for his mad running on the base paths. With no power to back him up he felt he had to get to third by hook or crook—by hit or steal—in order to be in position to score a run.

The third theory combined both the psychological and the practical. Yes, it was true that Willie might be doing better under the skillful hand-holding of Leo Durocher, but it was equally true that the burden of trying to carry the team was weighing on him too heavily. Maybe the feeling that the team was his burden to carry seemed like vanity, but the truth was the fans, the younger players, the manager and even Horace Stoneham did figure Willie as the man to lead the way. So there was nothing wrong with Willie that a little help wouldn't cure. If the Giants would wake up, Willie would wake up with them.

Whether with Willie in mind or not, the Giants did try to get help. In June they traded Lockman, Dark, Don Liddle and Ray Katt to the Cardinals for Red Schoendienst, Bill Sarni, Jackie Brandt and Dick Littlefield. Schoendienst, one of the league's finest second basemen, turned out to be a good investment, but on the whole the trade did little to change the Giants' position. By the All-Star game in July, that position was eighth—the bottom of the league.

The Giants could get no lower, positionally or in morale. Then, in a game in St. Louis, Willie hit a high pop fly along the first base line. Catcher Hal Smith went out after it, circling in foul territory. Willie stood by, watching. Suddenly a shift in the wind blew the ball fair and Smith had to chase it into fair territory to make the catch. Willie never moved from home plate. In the press box and in the grandstand there were murmurs of surprise at Willie's failure to run out the ball.

In the clubhouse after the game manager Rigney was fuming. He called Willie into his office and laced into him. "You ought to know better than that!" he stormed. "Suppose Smith had dropped the ball? We lost the game by plenty, but we were only a run behind then. How would you have looked if Smith had dropped it and thrown you out and then we lose by one run? You realize you would have cost us a chance to win?

Willie stood with his head bowed. "You right, Skip. I should have run it out. I thought it was foul but I should have run it out."

"It's not your place to think maybe it's foul," Rigney said. "Next time run. And I'm fining you twenty-five bucks to help you remember."

Willie looked startled, but he gulped and nodded. "You right to fine me, Skip. I should have run it out."

Perhaps the tongue-lashing and the fine served as a necessary shock—if it did, it knocked down the Willie-needs-his-hand-held school of thought. Perhaps being in eighth place relieved some of the pressure, there being no place else to go but up. In either case, or combination of cases, Willie slowly began to unwind. It started with a three-run homer in August that beat the Cubs, 4–2. Then the Pirates were his victims as he belted a triple and two doubles that drove in five runs for a 7–4 victory. And he broke out convincingly when the Dodgers came to the Polo Grounds in mid-August. First he beat them with a two-run homer, 3–1, then with a three-run homer, 10–9, then with another homer, 1–0.

The Reds came in next, and Willie won his fourth straight game with a homer, 5–3, also hitting two singles in that game. The next day he made it five straight wins and five straight home run days with a homer that made the difference in a 7–6 game.

129

The Giants moved out of the cellar into seventh place. The rest of the season was a slow run uphill. There was no time to make a success out of it; the best the Giants could do was rise to sixth. Toward the end they were playing well, playing together as a solidly welded unit, and it planted a seed of optimism for the next year. At the end Willie was running fastest of all. He finished with a .296 average, thirty-six home runs, eighty-four runs batted in, and forty stolen bases, tops in the major leagues.

12

It was apparent by the middle of May that the 1957 Giants had found their level in sixth place again. There was no reason to assume they could do better with their combination of fading oldsters and disappointing youngsters. Their luck was still running bad, besides. In spring training their three most promising young players, Jackie Brandt, Bill White and Willie Kirkland, were called into service. Catcher Bill Sarni suffered a heart attack and was lost for the season. Pitcher Johnny Antonelli, their one shining mound star of 1956, developed arm miseries and never regained his form.

They tried a couple of trades again. Thirty-eight-year-old Hank Sauer, a free agent released by the Cardinals, was picked up to play left field. Ray Jablonski and Ray Katt were obtained from the Cubs for Lennon and Littlefield. Whitey Lockman was repossessed from the Cardinals in exchange for Hoyt Wilhelm. Red Schoendienst, though he had done well in 1956, was considered expendable in exchange for Ray Crone, Danny O'Connell and the Giants' 1951 miracle man, Bobby Thomson, from the Braves.

This gave Rigney a patchwork line-up of Lockman at first,

O'Connell at second, rookie Andre Rodgers at shortstop, Thomson and Jablonski sharing third. Flanking Willie in the outfield were Sauer in left, Mueller in right. Valmy Thomas and Ray Katt were the catchers. Antonelli and Gomez headed the glaringly inadequate pitching staff, filled out with Al Worthington, Curt Barclay, Ray Crone, Stu Miller and Marv Grissom. Of these only relief pitcher Grissom could be counted on for any consistency.

As if the Giants hadn't enough troubles, a rasping voice out of the past came back to upset them further. In a national magazine article Leo Durocher blasted the Giants for mismanagement, particularly of Willie Mays. He told how he had treated Willie differently from the other Giants, exposing the fact that he had in effect pampered him and built him up to keep him playing at his peak. And he said that the Giants, including manager Rigney, had failed to capitalize on Willie's talents by neglecting him in this respect.

It was hardly a pronouncement calculated to inspire the staggering Giants, or Willie in particular. But Willie was up to the test.

"I got to admit the truth," he told a sports writer. "If I had come up to the majors with any other manager, I wouldn't be here now. Remember 1951, when Leo brought me up from Minneapolis? I started out going twenty-six for one, or something like that, and I asked him to send me down because I wasn't good enough. I was scared, I admit it. Any other manager, he'd of sent me down all right, and I'm telling you I'd never of come back. But Leo, he put words in my mouth and ideas in my head. He made me believe him. And that's why I'm here."

"You mean," the sports writer said, "that what Leo says was true? You did have to be pampered, built up all the time?"

Willie inclined his head in thought. "Well, I don't think Leo really pampered me, though I'm not mad at what he said.

I think if I'd made the same mistake twice he'd of fined me like anybody else. I just made sure not to make the same mistake twice. Now I don't want to get mixed up in any fuss about Leo and Rig. I play this game and I'll play it for any manager. Sure, the situation between me and Rig ain't the same as between me and Leo. But it ain't just because Rig is different. Me, I'm different too."

"How so?" came the question.

Willie shrugged. "A man grows up. He gets married. He gets responsibilities. When Leo was here, I had a problem I went to him. Who else could I go to? Sure, Leo was like a father to me. He liked me and I liked him. I was a young kid then. Leo wasn't only my manager. He was my friend. Now when I got a problem I talk it over with my wife. Maybe with Mr. Stoneham."

"Or with Rigney?"

"Look," Willie said. "I don't want to make it like I'd rather be playing for one manager than another. I don't want to make it look like I'm mad at Leo or Bill or anybody else. Leo's got a right to say whatever he wants. Sometimes a manager does have to use psychology on a player. Okay, so Leo used to tell me I was the greatest. I'm not saying I am, but who wouldn't like to hear those things? If it helped me, it didn't hurt anybody."

"Do you agree with Leo," the sports writer asked, "when he says you carried the Giants since you came up?"

Willie grinned. "Leo says a lot of things and sometimes it don't even mean anything. It's just for talking. I'm one man. There's nine on the team. They win plenty without me doing a thing.

"How about Leo's implying that some trades were made because certain players resented the special way he treated you?"

Willie grimaced. "Man, you touched a sore spot. I tell you something funny, but I ain't gonna answer that one directly.

133

As much as I liked having Leo backing me up so strong, I did worry about what some of the other guys might be thinking. And I tell you, I don't worry about it no more. Not with Rig. Last year I admit it was a little cool between us. Not that we didn't like each other or anything, because remember I played on the same team with him when I first came up. But we didn't give each other a chance. I was so worried about how he was going to treat me, you know, if he was going to get on me hard, and it turned out he was so careful to treat me the same as anybody that we never got together. This year it's different. We get along good; we know each other better."

"Has Rigney been helping you the day Leo did?"

"I don't need it," Willie said. "But if I had something I wanted to ask him, he'd help me, too. All he wants to do is win games. That's all I want. That's all everybody wants."

But the Giants were not winning consistently, and the fans stayed home in increasing numbers, or went to Yankee Stadium to watch the American League champions and their star center fielder Mickey Mantle. As apparent as the Giants' second division fate was the fact that they were no longer a paying attraction. A change of scenery was needed, and with the increasing tendency to shift major league franchises, the Giants late in May announced that in 1958 they would move to San Francisco. At the same time the Brooklyn Dodgers said they would be moving to Los Angeles, keeping the age-old feud between the two teams at least intrastate, if not intracity.

To most of the Giants the change in cities meant little emotionally. Only Willie had special memories. "After all," he said wistfully, "I never played no place else. After my aunt and my mother died this town was home to me, more so than Fairfield. New York was good to me, the fans were good to me. There's old Mrs. Goosby I'm gonna miss, and lots of friends around St. Nicholas Place."

134

"The kids and the stickball games?" someone suggested.

Willie chuckled. "Man, I don't get to play stickball no more. I'm a married man now you know." Then his eyes danced. "Hey, you think the kids in San Francsico play stickball?"

"Maybe the Say-Hey kid can teach them."

"You know," he said with a smile, "I don't think I've said 'say-hey' in a couple of years."

In June the Giants stirred themselves somewhat, rising briefly to fifth before dropping down again. Mostly the improvement was due to some timely hitting from newcomers Jablonski and Sauer who, together with Willie, managed to put out some kind of batting attack. In particular, Sauer was helping by taking some of the pressure off Willie, the pressure that had plagued him the year before. Though on the decline Sauer was still a threat to hit a home run any time. Therefore pitchers could no longer afford to give Willie bad balls to hit at, conceding him a walk if he refused to swing. With Sauer batting behind him, and hitting a fair share of homers, Willie had to be pitched to, and the results were reflected in his batting average. He was hitting .333 going into June.

On a twenty-one-game hitting streak he added more baseball veterans to his long string of admirers. By this time in his career Willie was a recognized streak hitter, but what made him different from most was that when he was slumping at the plate, he continued to dazzle in the field and on the bases. And when he got on a hot streak, like a clever gambler he capitalized on it, applying pressure to his opponents, forcing them into mistakes.

In a close game in Pittsburgh he provided the winning run that way. In the ninth inning he hit a sharp ground ball that bounced off the third baseman into short left field. It was a single, but noticing that the left fielder was a little slow coming in to field the ball, Willie kept right on going into second, making it a double. Then, after Sauer flied out, O'Connell bunted, but a little too sharply toward third. The third baseman fielded the ball quickly, started to throw to first, but hesitated a second when he realized that Willie was dangerous enough to try to make third on the throw. By the time the fielder made up his mind, O'Connell was safe, instead of being the second out, and Willie was on third. That set up the situation for Katt, who hit a short fly ball that should have been the third out. Instead, Willie tagged up and scored the winning run, despite a perfect throw by Roberto Clemente.

After the game, talking to Jim McCulley of the New York *Daily News,* Bobby Bragan, the Pirates manager, shook his head ruefully. "I never saw a guy who could beat you all by himself the way Willie does."

Bucky Walters, former pitching great of the Cincinnati Reds and now a new Giant coach, told a reporter, "Willie is the greatest player I've ever seen."

The next day Mays singled twice to drive in a pair of runs, then saved the game with another of his historical catches. Late in the contest, with two Pittsburgh runners on, Clemente hit a line drive straight for the right center field wall, over four hundred feet away. Willie turned instantly and just ran as fast as he could. At the last moment he threw himself up in the air, speared the ball, fell forward onto the ground, turned a complete somersault and came up holding the ball. In a flash he was on his feet, throwing the ball to second to hold the runners.

In the broadcasting booth, announcer Russ Hodges almost fell out the window in his excitement at describing the catch. "The greatest! Fantastic!" he screamed into the microphone. Later Giant coach Tommy Henrich, a great Yankee fielder himself in his day, and one who played alongside

136

Joe DiMaggio, called the catch a miracle. "It's the best catch I ever saw," he said, "bar none."

"Thank goodness Willie is having a great year," Giant president Stoneham added with a sigh. "If as a team we can't leave New York in style, at least let them remember us by Willie."

Mays continued his rampage. Against the Cubs he hit a three-run homer that tied the game, then in the ninth inning walked, stole second, stole third and scored the winning run when Cub catcher Cal Neeman threw the ball away. In Cincinnati he led a 17–7 rout of the Reds with two triples, two doubles, five runs batted in and two stolen bases. The next day he hit a homer over the left field scoreboard in Crosley Field, the first time it had ever been done.

On it went until the All-Star break, when for the fourth straight time Willie was named to the National League squad. After that he fell into his apparently annual slump, and it was then that there was proven to be a gap still in existence between him and manager Rigney, despite his earlier protestations to the contrary.

"I miss Stanky," he confided during his slump. "He would watch me, tell me if I was doing anything wrong. I always liked it when the veterans would tell me things. Stanky and Dark, they would always tell me. Now nobody tells me anything when I make a real bad play. I don't know why. Maybe they feel I'll resent it. A smart man, he don't resent it when somebody tries to help him. I take my orders, I try, but when I go bad, there's no one to tell me what to do."

He played himself out of the slump after a while and began to challenge Stan Musial and the Braves' Hank Aaron for the batting title.

Then finally it was September 29th, the last day for the New York Giants at the Polo Grounds. There was a big crowd on hand for the closing, and the fans didn't seem to care that the Giants lost, 9–1, to the Pirates. The crowd went wild after the game, overflowing onto the field, tearing bits and pieces which they could take home as souvenirs. There are a lot of memories imbedded into the steel and concrete of the Polo Grounds.

In the press box the writers, some of whom had sat in the same seat for thirty years covering the Giants, pulled together their own private mementoes. On a table there was a small pile of record books, the *Baseball Register, Who's Who in Baseball* and such, and there was a pang of regret as they realized that hereafter the Polo Grounds would exist only in those books.

A small farewell party was in progress in the clubhouse. All the Giant executives were there, and some of the great names in Giant history rubbed shoulders with the Giants who would be making history in a new city. Mel Ott and Carl Hubbell toasted their farewells and their wishes for success. Mrs. Blanche McGraw, widow of the famous John McGraw, greatest of all the Giant managers, dabbed at her eyes with a handkerchief. The party was being held in McGraw's old office.

Sipping a Coke off to one side, Willie looked around at the old pictures on the walls. There was one he recognized as McGraw raising a pennant flag, and there was another of McGraw, Babe Ruth and Walter Johnson. After a while Ott came over and congratulated him on his fine year. Musial had beaten him out for the batting title, but his own average had been .333. He had led the league in triples, with twenty, and with his twenty-six doubles and thirty-five homers had become the first National League player ever to hit more than twenty doubles, triples and homers in one season. Further, he had been the league's leading base stealer with thirty-eight.

He didn't remain long at the party; parties made him uncomfortable. When he left the Polo Grounds the field and the stands were long since empty, but in the street there were children still waiting for him. They yelled his name and pushed autograph books at him to sign. He scrawled his name, to the left and to the right, as he worked his way slowly to a waiting taxi.

Across the street two boys were playing catch. "Hey, Willie, look!" one of them shouted. He threw a ball into the air and the other boy stood there and made a basket catch.

New York was going to miss Willie Mays.

13

THE NEW OFFICE OF THE SAN FRANCISCO GIANTS WAS RICHLY appointed in leather and wood. From the broad expanse of window you could see San Francisco Bay, sparkling cold in the winter sunlight. Down to the right, in the middle of the bay, stood grim Alcatraz, and beyond it the broad span of Golden Gate Bridge straddling the harbor mouth. When you opened the window you could smell the Pacific, salty and clean, and if you closed your eyes and breathed deeply you could imagine the smells of Fisherman's Wharf, of chips and fried potatoes, see in your mind's eye the big red lobsters on their beds of crushed ice in the restaurant windows.

An interesting town, San Francisco—a town for gourmets and a town for jazz buffs; a town for sailors and a working-man's town; Joe DiMaggio's town and the town of Allen Ginsberg, who reads beatnik poetry to the North Beach set. It is cosmopolitan, sophisticated, yet also shirt-sleeved and warm, but Willie Mays got off to a bad start there because he is a Negro and he tried to buy a house in a white neighborhood.

The owner was willing to sell, and the real estate broker was willing, but some of the neighbors didn't like the idea and put pressures on them to withdraw their offer to him. Willie was hurt, but he didn't protest. However, some of his friends did, loud and long to the San Francisco newspapers. When the story broke, City Hall was deluged for hours with phone calls from citizens protesting the act, offering to sell Willie other homes in the city. Mayor George Christopher, indignant and embarrassed, said he would gladly share his home with Willie and his wife until they could find their own to buy. Willie phoned the mayor, expressed his gratitude for the offer, but said he preferred to stay with friends until something came along. The publicity and the apparent sincerity of the mounting indignation reversed the pressure, however, and the owner of the house agreed to sell. So in the middle of November, 1958, Willie and his wife moved into a beautiful $37,500 home on Miraloma Drive.

He discussed the incident with Horace Stoneham a couple of months later, as they sat in the office of the Giants' president. Stoneham wanted to know how he was getting along and Willie told him fine.

"Now that it's all over, the neighbors have calmed down," he said.

Stoneham nodded. "I hope you're not sore, Willie. It wouldn't pay to be sore at these people. They just don't know any better."

"I'm not mad at anybody," Willie said. "But talk about a thing like this goes all over the world and it sure looks bad for our country."

"Well, let's forget about unpleasant things today, Willie," the Giants' president said. "How about your new contract?"

"Whatever you say, Mr. Stoneham."

"You had a heck of a good year last year," Stoneham said.

Willie said, "You think so?"

Stoneham laughed. "Who's supposed to be convincing who around here?" He leaned across the desk. "You know, with the way Seals Stadium is laid out, you could hit four hundred there."

Willie grunted. "Me? I'm not a four hundred hitter."

"You're better than a four hundred hitter. You're a great team man. You deserve a raise, Willie. A fat raise. You got a figure in mind you want us to pay you?"

Willie shrugged. "You always treated me fair."

"How about seventy-five thousand dollars?"

Willie's eyes widened. "Seventy-five thousand! No kidding! Man, I never thought I could get that much."

Stoneham grinned. "You're some bargainer, Willie. It looks like I think more of you than you do of yourself."

"It ain't that, Mr. Stoneham," Willie said. "But I ain't no businessman, and like I said, you always treated me right. And seventy-five thousand dollars—that's a lot of money."

"Not so much. You know that during last season somebody offered us a million dollars for you?"

"A million dollars! Who that crazy man?"

"Frank Lane of the Cardinals. I told him if we moved to San Francisco and didn't take you with us the people out here would throw us all in the bay."

Willie laughed. Stoneham proffered a pen. Willie got up, walked to the desk and signed the contract that made him the highest paid player in Giant history.

He felt like a stranger in spring training, after returning to Phoenix from a Mexican tour of All-Stars. It was as though he had been traded over the winter. Manager Rigney was on hand, of course, among the familiar faces. Antonelli was there, too, also Westrum and Gomez and one or two others. But where were the rest of that wrecking crew that won the 1954 World Championship? Gone were Maglie, Stanky, Dark, Irvin, Thompson, Mueller and Wilhelm. But who were these young eager faces, these youthful figures bounding around the field in Giant uniforms? Rigney welcomed Willie back and introduced him around, but it took weeks for him to identify the faces with the names.

There was Leon Wagner, outfielder up from Danville in the Carolina League; Willie Kirkland, outfielder from Minneapolis in the American Association; Jim Davenport, third baseman also from Minneapolis; Orlando Cepeda, first baseman from Minneapolis; Felipe Alou, outfielder from Springfield in the Eastern League; Bob Schmidt, catcher from Minneapolis; a dozen others appeared briefly and disappeared as suddenly. Back from service were two more who had been rookies when they had been drafted—first baseman Bill White and outfielder Jackie Brandt.

Rigney himself seemed a bit bewildered by the overabundance of young talent in camp. He had known that the Giant front office had been digging desperately for young blood after the disasters of 1956 and 1957. They had traded and bought and planted seedlings among the minor league franchises they controlled or with which they had working agreements. Now the crop had come up a bumper. However, the big question was: Could you make a team out of a bunch of eager, inexperienced rookies?

"I don't have any choice," Rigney said when a reporter asked him the question. "I got to go with these kids. They're all I have. I got a hunch they'll be running the bases all year with their heads down, but at least they'll be running, and that's something the Giants haven't done for years. Besides, I think it's kind of appropriate. We're in a new city, starting off fresh. What could be better than starting off with practically a brand new team?"

Rigney's optimism was more for the press than for his private concern, however. Early in spring training he called Willie aside and asked for his help. "What do you think of these kids?" he began.

"Good lookin' bunch," Willie replied. "That Cepeda, he

143

can hit. Alou, someday he's gonna be one heckuva outfielder."

Rigney nodded. "This year, you're the take charge guy, Willie."

Willie stared at him. "Me? I'm no holler guy, Rig."

"Sure you are. Even if you don't know it. These kids look up to you, Willie. You're the big man on the Giants. In the league, too. You were the top man in the league before most of these kids even put on a professional uniform."

"Maybe so. But I can't boss nobody around, if that's what you want, Rig. I'm no good for that."

"I don't want you to boss anybody, Willie. That's my job," Rigney said. "But maybe a word to them here and there, you know. Kind of show them the way. Show 'em how a pro's supposed to act."

"Anybody ask me a question, I'm always willing to help."

"That's all I ask. We have a big job, Willie. It's kind of like we're on trial in Frisco. I think we have the makings of a fine team here. Nobody expects us to finish better than sixth again. With your help, with you leading the way, maybe we can pull a few surprises."

Willie nodded. "I do my best, Skip."

His best had always been superlative. But before the 1958 season was much more than a month old Willie was surpassing all his previous efforts. It began on May 9th, after three weeks of fast running by the Giants. With their rookies coming through they stayed up with the leaders and, to the amazement of the experts, were in second place on that day. But veteran baseball observers never put too much stake in fast starts by little regarded teams. They reasoned that the rookies would level off once the rest of the league warmed up and the Giants would then drop to their expected second division berth.

On May 9th, as the Giants came into Los Angeles for a four-game series with the Dodgers, they trailed the Milwaukee Braves by two games. And the "leveling off" predicted by the experts appeared to be starting. The Giants had dropped two straight games before this series, and now they trailed the Dodgers, 3–0, at the end of four innings.

In the fifth, after Johnny Antonelli and Eddie Bressoud had been retired, Alou singled off Dodger pitcher Don Drysdale. Spencer walked and up to the plate stepped Willie. Drysdale fed him a ball, then threw two fast balls past him for strikes. He tried another fast ball, and Willie slammed it deep into left center field for a home run.

That started the fireworks. With the score still tied, he hit another homer in the seventh with one man on base, then doubled in the ninth with bases loaded to give him seven runs batted in of an 11–3 victory.

The league had never seen such hitting, day after day. The Giants didn't win them all during Willie's streak. The rookies were spirited, but their inexperience showed through often enough to cost them ball games. A throw to a wrong base, poor base running, fumbles—these hurt in the close games. They lost one to the Cubs, 7–6, on a wild throw to third, despite the fact that Willie got four hits that day. The Braves beat them when a runner foolishly went past the third base coach's stop sign and was tagged out at the plate with the tying run. That day Willie had hit two homers and stolen two bases.

He helped them where he could, steadying them with his presence, pacing them with his skills. In the outfield he led Alou along, backing him up, giving the youngster plenty of room, building his confidence. Often on fly balls hit to left center field that were easy catches for him, Willie, watching left fielder Alou racing madly toward the ball, would drift out of his way and let him make the catch. Alou was asked about Willie one day, and the young fly chaser grinned. "He fine fellow that Willie. Help me all the time. Let me catch plenty of fly balls should be his."

Rigney went further in his praise. "Willie's really carrying those kids out there," he remarked to a sports writer one day. "Watch him catch a fly ball. He just seems to suck those kids along with him. 'Come on,' he seems to be saying, 'watch me.' And they come on, watching him. The things he teaches them!" Rigney shook his head in wonder and admiration.

Willie's incredible hitting streak ran through the month of May and into June. On the wings of it the Giants took over first place, held it briefly, lost it, regained it and see-sawed with it. Their problem was readily seen—inexperience and lack of solid pitching. After Antonelli there was nobody to be counted on. Gomez, Mike McCormick, Ramon Monzant, Stu Miller and Al Worthington comprised the bulk of the rest of the staff, and they were having trouble putting together two complete games in a row. Only Willie's hitting carried them through.

On June 6th, for example, Willie homered and singled his first two times up to give Ramon Monzant a 3–0 lead over the Reds. Despite another single and run batted in by Willie, however, Monzant lost the game 5–4, when he blew up in the sixth inning and allowed all the Cincinnati runs to score. The loss dropped the Giants to second place, behind the Braves, although at that point Willie was batting a phenomenal .432.

And the next day Willie stopped hitting.

As quickly as that, and just as completely.

He went three days without a hit. Worse, he couldn't lift the ball out of the infield. He couldn't figure out what was wrong, except that suddenly he seemed to feel tired. "My arms feel like lead," he told a reporter. "When I'm at bat they just won't do what I tell 'em to do."

On the fourth day he got a single in four times at bat, and after the game, as the Giants were dressing in the locker room, he pulled over a stool and sat down next to rookie Felipe Alou.

"You know, I'm not hittin' em so good the past couple of days," he said to the youngster. Alou looked surprised; Willie had never spoken to him much off the field. "Aah, you come out of it, Willie," he said. "You too good a hitter to be in slump for long."

Willie shook his head. "I'm tired. I may have to be out a few days. If I do, you'll take over center field, you know."

Alou's eyes widened. "Hey, that's a tough job. I can't take your place, Willie. That too big a job for me."

"Man, that's no way to talk," Willie hissed at him, low so the other players wouldn't hear. "You can catch and throw as good as me any day. Okay, so the pitchers fool you once in a while. Heck, man, you gotta expect that your first year. Took me two years to wise up. But you can't go around thinking you ain't good enough. You gotta figure you're as good as anybody, or you never will be any good."

Alou nodded, but it was plain from the forlorn look on his face that he was unconvinced, that the prospect of replacing Willie in center field distressed him. Willie sighed and returned to his own locker to finish dressing. The next afternoon, during batting practice, he confided his problem to Hank Sauer, with whom he had become quite friendly since the veteran outfielder joined the team in 1957. "I'd like to sit down, to tell you the truth, Hank. I'm a tired man."

"Why don't you go to Rig?" Sauer asked.

Willie related his conversation with rookie Alou. "I tell you, Hank, I know I can do the job out in the field, help the team, even when I'm not hitting. I feel like I'd be letting some of the kids down if I asked to be benched."

"And you'd be right," Sauer said. "Maybe it's not fair to stick you with the problem, Willie, but you got it whether you like it or not. Maybe you don't see it the way I do, because I watch these kids' eyes when you're up there swinging, or catching a fly ball most fielders would give up on. I've seen that kind of look only a couple of times before, and I've

147

been kicking around the major leagues since 1941. The kids used to look that way at DiMaggio, at Williams, at Musial. That's what you are to this team, to these kids."

"Man, I'm no Musial, I'm no DiMaggio," Willie said.

"The heck you're not," Sauer said. "If you don't believe it, ask any one of a couple of dozen old-timers who've seen 'em all play. Like me, for instance."

Willie grunted. "I guess I got to keep going," he sighed. "I got to break out of it someday."

In the meantime the Giants lost five straight games. Willie was being fooled by pitches he usually murdered; he was breaking the backs of rallies by striking out, hitting into double plays. Finally he felt obliged to ask Rigney to be benched. "Maybe a day or two off will do me some good," he said.

Rigney frowned. "Let me think about it."

The next day, before the Giants' final game of a home stand, Rigney met him as he came on the field for batting practice. "What do you say?" he asked Willie. "How do you feel? What do you want to do?"

Willie knew the answer his manager wanted to hear. "I think I'll play."

Rigney sighed. "Let's let it go that way for a while longer. Tomorrow we go on the road. Maybe you'll break out. Every line-up I try to make out comes up with your name on it, Willie."

"Keep my name in it," Willie said, tight lipped. "Maybe I'll come out of this slump myself."

14

THE BLINDS ON THE WINDOWS WERE DRAWN, MAKING THE hospital room dark though it was midafternoon, so that Willie Mays could watch the Giants-Phillies game on television. He sat propped up in bed, two pillows behind him, at New York City's Harkness Pavilion. It had been the only way out, flying to New York, checking into the hospital under the care of his personal physician. It had been the only possible solution to his problem. He had remained in the line-up in Pittsburgh, getting but one infield single. When the big chance came in the game he had struck out. Rigney then had agreed to bench him, but the next day had used him as a pinch hitter in the tenth inning and he had struck out again.

That had finished it, as far as Willie was concerned. He simply told Rigney he was tired, sick, that he was flying to New York for a physical examination and would rejoin the team in Philadelphia. Now here he was, in his second day at Harkness Pavilion, looking at the Giants lose another one to the Phillies. He watched in anguish as the uncertainty of the young players showed itself, as they committed glaring defensive lapses, failed to take advantage of opportunities on the attack.

149

The game ended. He slid out of bed, turned off the set, returned to sit in silent torture. He tried to keep his mind blank, to deny entry to the thoughts that swirled round and round, dizzying him, pounding at his senses. He fought them off—but they burned through.

Don't they think I'm human! the protest screamed within him. Don't they think I need help? Don't they think I want somebody to tell me what I'm doing wrong? Everybody tells me what a big man I am. I'm DiMaggio. I'm Musial. The kids look up to me. They depend on me. These kids, they're twenty-four, twenty-five years old, some of them. Me, I'm only twenty-seven. What they want from me?

The doctors stick me full of needles. Checking blood. Don't have to check my blood. I'm tired, that's all. I know what's wrong with me. I need somebody. I need somebody older over me, someone who knows all about me and where I came from and how it was when I came up. You know what I could use? Jackie. Yeah, if I had Jackie Robinson. One year, that's all I would need. One year for Jackie to play with me and tell me things. He'd tell me. He'd watch me, and he'd tell me.

That's the trouble. They're afraid to tell me anything. Nobody tells me nothing. What they afraid of? Maybe they think I'd resent it. Why should I resent it? I got a lot to learn yet and I want to learn it. Man's gotta be crazy resenting it when somebody tells him something that's maybe gonna help him.

Willie snapped on the light. He tried to read. It was no good. The thoughts returned.

Sauer. He's the only one. Maybe because he's been around so long he knows how it is. He ain't scared to tell me things. He's a good guy. But I need somebody who knows me better. Like Jackie. He knew me when I came up. I learned just watching him. Imagine what I could learn if he was here to tell me things? Like when a ball's hit and I'm running. I

150

do what I saw Jackie do a lot. I put my eyes where the ball is. I watch it. The outfielder don't throw—I run. He fumbles, I run. Can't wait for the coach to tell you. And you can't stop to look. Just a peek while you're running. I learned that from Jackie.

Some guys hit .350, they don't care about nothing. Me, I'm still hitting about .380. But only five hits last thirty-six times up. Man, that drives me crazy.

He got up then and turned the television set back on, searching for a western movie. He got one and returned to bed, hoping the movie would conquer the brooding thoughts. It was good for a few moments, then they came back again, unabated.

I ain't much of a worrier, but I'm human, too. I love this game. I got to play, got to do things every day. But I need somebody older, need somebody to tell me things. Like Leo used to. Leo used to talk to me all the time when he thought I needed it. He used to tell me to sit next to him on the bench and he'd just keep talking. Now there ain't nobody. I got to find out myself what's wrong. It ain't right. They think I don't need help but I'm only a human being, same as everybody.

He got up and switched off the television set. The western movie was no help. He tried the radio on the night stand next to the bed. The music was loud, blaring, jumpy. He shut it off, lay back against the pillows and stared at the ceiling. He lay there like that, until the sunlight that filtered through the blinds turned gray, until a nurse came and wheeled in his dinner.

He rejoined the club two days later in Philadelphia; there was nothing wrong with him physically. He knew the medical report would confirm that, but he hoped that perhaps the short rest, being away from baseball for a few days might refresh him. Rigney greeted him diffidently. "The docs find

151

out anything?" he asked. Willie shook his head. "It was like I said. I needed a rest, is all."

"We needed you in there," Rigney said. "The kids. They feel better with you in there."

"I'm better now," Willie said. "Don't know if those hits'll come back right away. But I feel better. I'm rested."

The hits didn't come back right away, as Willie had feared, but he contrived to beat the other teams with his different skills. The night he returned he got a single and walked once, but each time he was on base he stole second and scored, leading the Giants to a 5–4 victory.

His fielding was as miraculous as ever. To the New York baseball writers who had come along to cover the Giants in their new home, his fielding gems were by now in the nature of being routine, but the San Francisco writers marveled at every spectacular play. When Willie made an exceptional catch, there ensued some humorous byplay among the various writers. While the San Franciscans would leap up in amazement, the New Yorkers would regard the scene with studied calm. "Hey!" a San Francisco writer would cry, "didn't you guys see that catch Willie made?" And the New Yorker would feign a yawn. "Oh, that! I've seen him make better ones every day since 1951."

But even the New Yorkers had to stand up and cheer one day during Willie's continued batting slump. At the plate for the Phillies was Jim Hegan for his first National League at-bat since being obtained from the Cleveland Indians. Hegan caught one of Ramon Monzant's pitches and hit it over four hundred feet to left center. Back went Willie, running out from under his cap. He turned once, caught a peek at the ball, turned and ran some more. Finally he leaped up and caught the ball against the wall. Slamming into the barrier, he bounced off, hit the ground and rolled over, and came up holding the ball aloft, grinning.

The crowd stood up and cheered along with the sports

writers and Willie's teammates, while Hegan walked back to the bench, scuffing at the dirt, growling at his bad luck. The next time he came up to hit there were men on first and second. This time he looped a short fly into center field. It looked like a sure Texas leaguer hit. The runners went halfway down the base lines, wary of Willie, as Hegan ran confidently to first. But charging in from deep center field, Willie never stopped trying. He ran with his body low, head forward, leaned down at the last moment to make a shoestring catch of the ball, and in the same motion straightened and threw a line drive to the second baseman to complete a double play.

The crowd was beside itself with wonder. The San Francisco writers shook their heads in awe. The New York writers exchanged secret smiles. Hegan stomped back to the bench and threw himself down. "When they beat us in the 1954 World Series I figured at least I'd never have to look at that guy Mays again," he wailed to his teammates. "But now look! How can you guys stand playing against him twenty-two games a year?"

Willie's long batting slump continued, however. From a high point of .432 on June 6th he slid downward rapidly and steadily until as August arrived he was down to .320. As many a baseball observer was quick to point out, .320 could hardly be considered "down," except for the fact that it was a drop of more than one hundred points during a two-month stretch of hitting at about a .240 pace. Fortunately for the Giants, Willie's presence on the field meant as much as his hitting prowess, as Rigney understood, and as Willie himself modestly admitted. While the pitching staff blundered through the summer months, the rookies, led by Willie's example, maintained the Giants' third place position. Everyone in the league waited for their collapse. Instead, Willie began to hit again, and the league shuddered.

He got hot with the bat as suddenly and inexplicably as

he had gotten cold. And coincidentally—or perhaps in the psychology of it, it was more than a coincidence—he began to hit again right after the Giants suffered their worst setback of the season.

The setback began in Cincinnati on the night of July 31st. The Giants were still in strong running for the league leadership, battling with the Braves. That night at Cincinnati, however, they lost, 10–9, after leading, 9–4, as late in the game as the eighth inning. Worse than the actual loss was the fact that Rigney threw five pitchers into the game trying to save it, and the next day the Giants opened in Milwaukee for four games in three days.

The pitchers weren't up to it, as thin and weak as the staff was even in prime physical shape. Where early in the season Willie's phenomenal hitting was able to overcome their deficiencies, this time there was no salvation. The Giants lost the four games, and for all practical purposes any chance they had at winning the pennant.

They were a disconsolate group as they flew to Chicago, and Willie the most disconsolate of all. On the plane Rigney slid into a seat next to him, knowing that should the letdown feeling get out of hand the Giants might continue to drop right through into the second division. He tried to shake Willie out of it. "Forget Milwaukee," he told him. "We can't do anything about it any more. Tomorrow's another day. You used to say that yourself, Willie."

"Used to say a lot of things," Willie grunted. "Don't say 'em much any more."

"Listen, Willie, if you let this get you down, these kids are gonna go right down with you. If you get up and fight, they'll get up with you. Which way would you rather see it?"

Willie didn't answer. Instead, he shut his eyes and pretended to sleep.

The next day in Chicago he gave Rigney his answer. He came up for his first at bat with a man on second and the

Giants trailing, 2–0. Taylor Phillips, the Cubs' pitcher, tried him with a fast ball outside, then a curve that was good for a strike. Willie fouled off the next pitch for strike two. He stepped out of the batter's box, rubbed dirt on his hands, stepped back in again. Phillips came down with another fast ball. Willie swung. The ball jumped, arced far to left center field and landed deep into the stands for a home run. It was his first homer in more than a month.

That tied the score, and on the bench Rigney chewed his lips nervously. If Willie came out of his slump, anything might happen with this team. If only the pitching—but his pitchers were failing him again. Gomez was knocked out of the box in the fifth inning, and the Cubs went ahead, 4–2. In the sixth Willie singled home O'Connell from third and promptly stole second. Cepeda, the next batter, hit a slow roller to shortstop and beat it out for a hit. Willie didn't stop at third, however. While the Chicago infield dawdled with the ball he sped around third base and headed for home. Suddenly the Cubs woke up. First baseman Dale Long, who had been aimlessly holding the ball after getting the late throw from shortstop, fired home. In his haste he threw wildly. Willie came across the plate standing up. Cepeda wound up on third and scored after a fly ball to put the Giants in front, 5–4. It was enough to win, but to make sure, Willie hit another run home in the eighth inning for a 6–4 victory.

The win moved the Giants into second place ahead of the Pirates, but still four games behind the league-leading Braves.

Willie worked his way back slowly after that, lifting the team right along with him. It didn't show in the league standings because the Braves were too tough to catch and the Giant pitching so bad that it caused their eventual slide to third place. Nevertheless there was a buoyancy apparent, a surge of good feeling that spread throughout the team—

155

youngsters and veterans alike—when Willie began to hit again. For they knew that what a San Francisco reporter had written that summer was true. "As Willie Mays goes, so go the Giants. Their fortunes are inextricably interwoven with his."

The Giants finished third, twelve games behind the Braves, but on an upbeat note. Had the pitching been different, the entire season would have had to be re-written. "When Willie began hitting again we were close enough to catch up," manager Rigney said after the season's final game. "But the pitching was worse this year than it was in '56 and '57, when we finished sixth. We made it third this year on Willie's hitting and the performance of some great kids."

Mays wound up with a .347 average, second best in the league behind Richie Ashburn of the Phillies, who hit .350. He hit twenty-nine home runs, batted in ninety-six and again led the league in stolen bases, with thirty-one.

The Giants considered the 1958 season a huge success. In their debut at San Francisco, they had astonished the experts who had predicted the second division for them. They had played to capacity crowds at Seals Stadium and on the road as fans flocked to watch Willie and an exciting group of colorful rookies. President Stoneham was so pleased he raised Willie's salary again—to $80,000, as much money as Babe Ruth ever received in one season.

"A swell present, especially since me and Marghurite just adopted a two-week-old baby boy," Willie announced to Stoneham. "Named him Michael. Someday he can take over for me in center field," he chuckled.

But Stoneham shook his head. "Willie, nobody could ever take your place in center field."

THE HOT STOVE LEAGUE IS AS OLD AS BASEBALL ITSELF. IT GOT
its name from the potbellied iron stoves that stood in the
old general stores of the small towns. In the winters the town
cronies would gather in the store and warm their hands
around the stove, meanwhile exchanging gossip, spinning
tales, swapping stories, and inevitably, comparing the merits
of the nation's athletes. It was for this reason that a New
York sports columnist nicknamed winter baseball talk the
Hot Stove League.

In the winter of 1958-1959 the talk was about Willie Mays
and Mickey Mantle, the star center fielder for the New York
Yankees. Like Willie, Mantle had been brought up to the
major leagues during the 1951 season, and since then had
been heralded as one of the great players of the game. Naturally each had his own boosters when their merits were compared. But aside from the partiality of their fans, there were
more objective views and comparisons being made continually by professional baseball observers. Sometimes these comparisons were made in public print, sometimes in Manhattan's own peculiar version of the Hot Stove League, the din-
ing room at Toots Shor's popular restaurant, frequented by
sports figures and Broadway celebrities.

Sitting around a table one evening were Dizzy Dean, the former pitching great of the St. Louis Cardinals' "Gas House Gang," Buddy Blattner, a former Giant infielder, and Mel Ott, one of the all-time Giant greats. The three men now were baseball broadcasters—this was just weeks before Ott's tragic death in an automobile accident—and they were on the much-discussed baseball topic of the day: Willie Mays versus Mickey Mantle. All agreed that both players were potential Hall of Famers, but then Dean added, "Still, if I had to pick one of them I'd rather pitch against, it would be Mantle. You could strike him out more often. Not that you wouldn't want to have both of them on your ball club, but one might be a little better than the other defensively— Mays. I'd have to say he's the better fielder all the way around."

"I'll go along with that," Blattner said.

"As far as hitting goes," Dean continued, "Mantle hits the longer ball. There's no question about that. But I don't think he's as consistently tough at the plate as Mays."

"His physical condition may have something to do with that," Ott said. "Remember he has bad knees."

"You have to consider that when you compare two players as to their value to a club. Mantle hits the longer ball but you have to figure he's liable to go out there any day and get hurt and end his career. All around I'd have to say Mays is the boy."

Blattner nodded. "Besides the advantage of being physically sound, Mays is the only ballplayer who can beat you four ways—arms, legs, glove and bat. You know, Stan Musial always said he wasn't a complete ballplayer because he couldn't throw. Well, it's good enough for him, but Mays has everything. Mantle, I would say, doesn't have quite the glove and not quite the arm."

"He does have speed," Dean said.

"Yes," agreed Blattner. "But he can't take the risk. You

158

can't gamble a million-dollar ballplayer for a stolen base. That's what it comes down to. Mays, at least so far, has shown that he can take the beating."

"True," Dean said. "He really slams into a base." He chuckled. "And that cap of his always flys off doin' it."

"That's another important thing," Blattner said. "Color. Willie has a flair for it. Now Mantle, he's graceful in everything he does. But his color comes when he swings the bat. Mays, he'll run out from under his cap; he'll force you into errors by the way he runs the bases; he uses the most beat up old glove you ever saw and he makes those basket catches at his belt buckle. It's just color. And brains. Willie may not have much school education, but in baseball he's got a Master's degree in both pockets. Baseball is simple for him. When they hit it he's supposed to catch it. When they throw it he's supposed to hit it."

"What do you say, Mel?" Dean addressed Ott. "You haven't said too much about either of these boys."

"I tell you, I haven't seen Mays play as much as you two have—maybe eight or nine times altogether. So I don't think I'm entitled to an opinion. But I can say this. Every place I go in baseball, I hear Mays. They tell me he's the far superior ballplayer. More exciting, more everything. One of those players that comes along only once in a very great while."

Despite opinions such as these, despite the years of spectacular exhibitions at the Polo Grounds, despite a fine season in 1958, Willie was regarded as something less than a hero in San Francisco. Perhaps part of it might have been because of those very attributes and high praise mentioned earlier. For there is a certain perversity among many sports fans causing them to delight in the failures of popular favorites. There is a "knock-down-the-favorite" streak running through these fans. Especially is this true when the favorite is not one of their own choice—as Willie Mays was not to fans in San

Francisco. Humph, here comes that big man from New York, ran through many minds. Let's see how good he really is. Let Willie falter for a moment and the boos descended upon him, as they did with some regularity in 1958.

Willie was a Polo Grounds hero and a Polo Grounds hero he would always be. He won grudging respect from the fans and from the San Francisco writers—admiration, even. But to the regulars at Seals Stadium the cheers were reserved for their own heroes, the new Giant players who were making their major league debuts and their reputations in San Francisco. These were "their own." Orlando Cepeda, "Rookie of the Year" in 1958 and winner of San Francisco's first Giant popularity poll conducted by a local paper, was foremost among these heroes. Then there was Jackie Brandt, Willie Kirkland, Felipe Alou and the others.

There was this much truth: In Seals Stadium Willie was not the Willie the San Franciscans had heard and read about. Missing were some of the miracle catches that were his trademark, and after looking and waiting for them through all of 1958, the fans began to doubt. The fact was, however, that the physical layout of Seals Stadium made such fielding acrobatics impossible. In the Polo Grounds Willie could—and would—run a mile to deep center to pull down a ball. In Seals Stadium the ball bounces off the scoreboard or falls into the bleachers before Willie even gets up steam. There is no running room in Seals Stadium for Willie.

Strangely, even so-called professional observers have overlooked this in San Francisco. "The best outfielder I ever saw in Seals Stadium," a local announcer once remarked, "was Tom Umphlett," and this was a reference to an outfielder who had failed to stick in the major leagues. When manager Rigney heard the remark, he shook his head sadly. "There isn't enough ground behind Willie to show these people what he's really like," he said. "But somehow they just don't realize that, just as they don't realize how many other things

160

Willie does for a team to help it win. For example, if he really cared, he still could make sensational catches like he used to. Remember in the old days he used to play between guys like Mueller and Sauer and Dusty Rhodes—no disrespect meant to those guys—and he'd just have to go over into left and right field and make sensational catches. Now he has Brandt and Alou flanking him, and these kids have the range to catch the ball themselves. Willie still gets over there, but now he gets out of the way and lets these kids make the catch, always backing them up just in case."

Nevertheless, San Francisco appeared ready to believe the worst about Willie. It was a strange misalliance, as one New York sports columnist observed. Willie was always ready to like everybody, but everybody was not ready to like him. The San Francisco sports writers didn't help the situation, either. Perhaps they expected a certain glibness from Willie. Perhaps, knowing only one other baseball hero of such magnitude—native son Joe DiMaggio—they didn't know how to talk to Willie. They would ask him, "Describe some of the great catches you made," and he would shrug, "Man, I can't describe 'em, I was too busy catchin' 'em. Ask somebody who was watching me." The writers would take this for sullenness, or worse, snobbishness, where those who knew Willie from the beginning would recognize it as another demonstration of his absolute honesty and modesty.

Or perhaps he would have a big day, get three hits, steal a couple of bases. A local reporter would ask eagerly, "Would you say this was the best day you've had this year?" And Willie would reply, "Don't talk about that. I'm superstitious. Talk about how many hits I got and the next day I don't get none."

The reporter would walk away mumbling that Willie was a prima donna, a tough man to talk to. He would print his opinion, and there were many who were glad to accept it as truth and boo Willie at the ball park. Did Willie resent it?

161

Certainly he was hurt, but he refused to discuss it with anyone, even to a New York sports writer, an old friend, who visited him during spring training in 1959. "I don't want to make a big thing out of it," he said to the writer. "I'm going to be playing in San Francisco a long time. Besides," he added with typical generosity, "it ain't the people who come out every day who boo me, just the ones who come out once in a while, and they only remember the mistakes they saw me make last time they came around."

Willie was sitting on a stool in front of his locker in the Phoenix clubhouse, rubbing his stomach, where the slightest suggestion of a bulge was beginning to show. He chuckled when the reporter remarked about it. "Guess I'm getting old," he said. The laugh had none of the high-pitched giggle that had distinguished it in his earlier years; it was deeper, more reflective. Not quite twenty-eight years old, he had become the elder statesman of the Giants.

He sat there in the clubhouse watching the parade of youngsters swirl around him, youngsters whom he dated for the most part by only three or four years. But he had spent those few years starring for the team, and that made the difference. He looked at the firm body of one of the youngest Giants, pitcher Mike McCormick, who stood toweling himself at the locker next to his. "He's got it made," Willie said, motioning toward McCormick. "Twenty years old and his whole life ahead of him."

It appeared in the spring of 1959 that the Giants themselves had it made. Third place finishers the year before with a terrible pitching staff and a line-up of rookies, they had improved themselves with their year of experience and important winter trades. Gone were virtually the last of the old Giants, with the exception of Mays and Antonelli. Gomez and Valmy Thomas had been traded to the Phillies for pitcher Jack Sanford. Grissom and Bill White were traded to the Cardinals for pitcher "Sad Sam" Jones. Lockman was sold to the Baltimore Orioles.

The 1959 roster shaped up as one of the youngest in baseball, and potentially one of the most dangerous. At first base was Orlando Cepeda, who hit .312 and twenty-five homers in 1958; at second Daryl Spencer; at shortstop Andre Rodgers and Eddie Bressoud were rival candidates, while at third base was Jim Davenport. The outfield had Mays, Alou and Brandt, with Willie Kirkland, Hank Sauer and Leon Wagner as alternates. Catching was Bob Schmidt, backed up by Hobie Landrith. The pitching staff was led by Antonelli, followed by Jones, Sanford, Curt Barclay, Paul Giel, McCormick, Stu Miller, Ramon Monzant and Al Worthington.

On hand for tryouts in Phoenix were a number of minor leaguers who hoped to get the call later in the season should the Giants need help. Among these was a six-foot four-inch first baseman who impressed Willie so much he pointed him out to manager Rigney. On the field one day, as this youngster was batting, Willie nudged his manager. "Take a look at that Willie McCovey," he said. "Man, he hits the ball a mile."

Three weeks after spring training began, Giant hopes for 1959 plummeted to near despair. It happened in Scottsdale, Arizona, where they were playing an exhibition against the Boston Red Sox. In the sixth inning, with the Giants leading, 3–2, Willie doubled with one out. Spencer, the next batter, took two called strikes. On the next pitch Willie tried to steal third. He had it made easily, and when at the last moment Spencer tapped the pitch slowly toward shortstop, he turned third and headed for the plate. Don Buddin, the Red Sox shortstop, raced in on the infield grass, fielded the ball with his bare hand and threw to catcher Sammy White, who took the erratic throw on the first base side of the plate. But as he reached he kept his left leg extended to the plate. Sliding in safely, Willie collided with the catcher's shin guard. His right leg was ripped open from ankle to knee.

163

He lay there stunned for a moment, not realizing the seriousness of his injury. But as he rose he saw the blood rushing from the wound, and his teammates noticed it at the same moment. They rushed from the dugout and helped him into the clubhouse. Trainer Frank Bowman examined the gaping wound, winced, cleaned and dressed it, then said crisply, "Somebody better take him to the hospital. He's gonna need stitching."

"I'll drive him," pitcher Curt Barclay volunteered. "I got my car right outside." Sauer and Jablonski helped him carry Willie outside, as Rigney stood by, white faced. Then Barclay sped to the South Phoenix hospital. As he drove, the youngster couldn't help asking one question. "Willie, one thing I can't understand. It was only an exhibition game. Why'd you take the chance of hurting yourself? You could have held up at third and played it safe."

Willie shrugged. "If I don't do it right in training, I can get into bad habits for later."

Barclay pondered the thought a moment, staring straight ahead as he drove, his brow wrinkling. Then he nodded, as though he had suddenly learned a great truth.

The hospital had been alerted by a phone call from the stadium, and nurses brought a wheel chair to the car. They wheeled Willie into the emergency room, where a doctor removed Bowman's temporary bandage, took a long look, whistled, then went to work with the sutures. When he finished, Willie had thirty-five stitches in his leg. "You were open clear down to the shinbone," the doctor told him.

The details didn't interest Willie. He had one thing in mind. "Can I play tomorrow?" he asked.

The doctor stared at him. "Tomorrow! You better lay off using that leg for two weeks!"

Willie frowned. "Man, I can't sit down for two weeks. Never be in shape for opening day like that." He grabbed Barclay's arm. "C'mon, let's get out of here," he said, dragging the pitcher out to the car. They drove directly to the Giant training camp headquarters at Phoenix Municipal Stadium, where he knew the team would be after the game at nearby Scottsdale. Before Barclay could speak, Willie, walking into the locker room unaided, announced to Rigney, "Ready to play tomorrow, Skip."

"Hey!" Barclay protested. "The doc said you better stay out for two weeks."

Willie glared at him. "What you talkin' about, man. He never said that."

Rigney smiled. "Hey, Doc," he called to trainer Bowman, "take a look at Willie's leg."

"Better leave it alone for a day or two," Bowman said. "They do much sewing, Willie?"

"Thirty-five stitches," Willie said, a little proudly.

"No kidding, Willie, you better not try to play for at least a week, anyhow," Bowman told him. "If these stitches open up on you the leg can get infected. Then you're in bad trouble."

Willie sighed resignedly, but Rigney heaved a sigh of relief. "Whew! It could have been a lot worse. I thought for a minute there in Scottsdale you might not be ready for opening day."

"I'll be ready, Skip," Willie said grimly.

16

In the clubhouse at Seals Stadium, the morning of open-ing day, Rigney was addressing the players, and as he took off his cap Willie was shocked as he noticed for the first time that his manager's hair was snowy white. Why, he can't be more than forty-one or so, Willie thought. Man, what being the manager of a baseball team can do to you. He felt a sudden sympathy for Rigney, a warmth of understanding he had never felt before. Rigney was saying:

"We have a pennant-contending ball club here. We're young, we're going to make mistakes. But if we don't make the same mistakes twice, we can go all the way."

Just like Mr. Leo used to say, Willie thought.

But the season was hardly a week old before Rigney despaired of a pennant. The Giants weren't too badly off judged merely by the standings of the clubs. They were in third place, not far from the league-leading Braves and Dodgers, but how they weren't in the cellar Rigney couldn't understand. Youth, their major strength and at the same time their glaring weakness, had betrayed them. In their first nine games they committed eighteen errors, sixteen of them in the infield and twelve around the vital second base-shortstop positions. Andre Rodgers made eight of them; Spencer made three in one game. Besides the errors charged in the books, there were glaring errors of omission.

In one game against the Dodgers, for example, Junior Gilliam opened the fifth inning with a double. Norm Larker followed with a short fly into center, behind Spencer. Gilliam held up as Mays raced in for the sinking ball. He couldn't reach it, but scooped it up on the short bounce, feinted Gilliam back to second and then started to throw to first, where he had seen Larker take too wide a turn and head for second, thinking Mays was going to throw to third to get Gilliam. But Cepeda wasn't at first, having wandered off the bag toward the pitcher's mound. Willie now had gone too far with his throwing motion to check it. All he could do was throw somewhere—and he threw it home. But nobody was there, either. Catcher Schmidt just wasn't paying attention. The ball bounced past the plate, and by the time it was recovered Gilliam had scored and Larker was at third, from where he scored on a fly ball moments later.

As Willie trotted in to the dugout after the third out, a fan leaned out of the box seats and yelled at him. "Ya bum ya, where ya throwin' the ball?" The chorus was taken up, and soon the Seals Stadium boos descended upon Willie. For once the local writers were with him. One of them pointed out next day that far from its being an error on Willie's part, the throw only went to prove just how great a player Willie was. The logic was this: He had first made a running scoop of a base hit that would have done credit to a shortstop. Then, in full motion, he had bluffed Gilliam into holding second while at the same time, incredibly, he had noted that Larker had swung too wide and was trapped off first. Then, unable to throw to first because nobody was there, he had managed in mid-motion to switch his throw to home, where again the man who should have been there was absent.

167

What kept the Giants going amid all these fielding lapses was their hitting and pitching. Antonelli, Jones and Sanford started strongly, Antonelli winning three straight and Sanford pitching a one-hitter against the Cardinals. Davenport at one point got six hits in a row. Cepeda hit safely in the first nine games, including five homers and five doubles among his hits. Willie was hovering at the .300 mark and batting in important runs. The Giants had dropped two straight games and were losing their third straight before Willie rescued them. They were trailing the Cardinals, 1–0, in the third inning when Sanford walked, moved up on a sacrifice and scored the tying run on Willie's single. Then in the sixth inning, with the Giants holding a precarious 2–1 lead, Willie drove in two more runs with a bases-loaded single to insure the victory.

The following day Antonelli and the Red Birds' Larry Jackson were locked in a 1–1 duel for five innings. In the Giants' sixth Davenport singled and Brandt singled, bringing up Willie, who promptly smashed Jackson's first pitch through the box. Don Blassingame, making a great play behind second, came up with the ball, couldn't get Willie, but threw to second in time to force Brandt, robbing Willie of a hit. Still, on the force-out Davenport scored the tie-breaking run, and two innings later Willie made it 3–1, singling home Davenport from second. That clinched Antonelli's victory.

The Giants dropped two straight again after that, losing to the Dodgers in Los Angeles, before Willie broke out with a triple and a single in the third game to win another for Sanford, 5–1.

Back in Seals Stadium after the Dodger series, Willie continued hitting, with Cepeda behind him helping to pace the attack. The Giants moved up to second place, and the San Francisco ball park rang with cheers. But the cheers were notably for Cepeda, for Alou, for Brandt. At best Willie got a scattering of applause, and at worst the jeers were quick to come. One night, with runners on second and third, the enemy pitcher began to walk him intentionally. But the fourth ball was pitched a little close and Willie reached out, trying to place-hit a single that would have scored two runs. Instead, he popped out, and the boos rained down upon his head.

In the locker room later, he tried to shrug it off. "I made a mistake," he admitted. "The people here don't let me forget it when I make a mistake. I'm the same guy who got the hits yesterday, but it's what I do today that counts."

The next day the Phillies came to Seals Stadium and were demolished by Willie, who helped win two out of the three games with a home run, a triple, three doubles, three singles, three stolen bases and eight runs batted in. Then Cincinnati came in to town for three games. Brooks Lawrence started the opener against Antonelli, and had a 2–1 lead going until the fifth inning. Then he walked Andre Rodgers, who had become the Giants' new lead-off man. Kirkland singled and Mays walloped a home run. That finished Lawrence, and the Giants went on to win, 9–2, Willie adding two singles later in the game.

In the second game Don Newcombe, former Dodger pitching ace, opposed Stu Miller. The Reds scored first on a homer by Vada Pinson, their young center field star, but the Giants came back in their half on a lead-off homer by Rodgers, a walk to Kirkland, a run-scoring double by Willie, who scored himself a moment later on a single by Wagner. The Reds tied it in the fifth on a single and a homer by Newcombe, an excellent hitting pitcher. In the Giant half of that inning, however, Willie followed a single by Rodgers with a home run, putting the Giants in front, 5–3. That would have been enough, for Miller steadied the rest of the way, but to make sure the Giants added four more runs in the eighth when with two out Kirkland walked, Willie doubled, Wagner tripled and Cepeda homered.

The Giants were looking strong, sitting in second place, trailing the Braves by three games. Many of the early season bugs were being ironed out. The line-up was shaping into a solid offensive and defensive unit, thanks to some intricate juggling by manager Rigney. In the face of criticism he had persevered with shortstop Rodgers and prospered. The youngster seemed to be overcoming his jitters, was fielding well and, moved up to the lead-off position, hitting as Rigney knew he could. Cepeda, benched for three days during a slump, had been ably replaced by Jablonski and had come back strongly against Cincinnati. Alou and Brandt, right-hand hitters, were occasionally being alternated with Wagner and Kirkland, who were left-hand hitters, and with good results. The pitching staff, cause of the previous year's grief, looked like one of the best in the league.

And Willie, boos notwithstanding, was hitting .346, and an important .346, as shown when it was compared with the average of the Braves' Hank Aaron, leading the league with an astronomical .477. Yet despite the vast difference in their averages, Willie had actually scored five more runs than Aaron, thirty to twenty-five, and had batted in just three less, thirty-two to thirty-five. In short, Willie was hitting and getting on base when it counted the most.

The Giants had reason for optimism, as the Braves came in for three games. It was early in the season, only the end of May, but it was a kind of test. Observers already had pointed out that the surprising Giants seemed to be the Braves' only serious rivals for the pennant. This three-game series could go a long way toward showing exactly how serious a threat the Giants were.

Warren Spahn was the Braves' choice to open the series; Jones was picked to pitch for the Giants. For three innings the game was scoreless. Then, in the fourth, the Braves scored on a double and a single. In the Giant half of the inning, Spahn retired Rodgers and Wagner, but Willie poled a towering homer into the left field seats to tie the score. But the Braves knocked Jones out in the sixth inning on two singles and a double, going on to win, 4–2.

The next game was a rout. The Braves scored four times in the first inning to chase pitcher Sanford, then added four more later off the Giants' relief pitchers. Final score: Braves eight, Giants one. The Giants' lone run came across with Willie, who singled, stole second and scored on a single by Brandt. The Giants were five games behind now, tied for third place with the Dodgers.

The final game of the three-game set was a vital one. Another loss would not only put the Giants six games behind, a serious gap even at this stage of the season, but it might so affect the spirit of the young players that they would collapse completely.

Willie was waiting to take his practice swings before game time, standing off to the side of the batting cage, when Rigney came to him. The Giants' manager didn't say much, just, "Big one today, Willie," but the worried look in his eyes said more. Willie noticed the lines around the other man's eyes, the fringes of white around the baseball cap.

"We win it, don't worry, Skip," he said quietly.

They won it. They won on some clutch relief pitching by Sam Jones in the ninth inning, and on clutch hitting by Willie, who drove in three runs with two doubles; three runs that made the difference in the 6–3 victory.

Willie saved the Giants from disaster, but the test had not favored the Giants' chances. A week later, in Milwaukee, they had another opportunity in a four-game set, having fought back to within two games of the Braves. Joey Jay and Sam Jones battled scorelessly for two innings in the first game, then with two out in the third, Willie started a rally with a double. Cepeda followed with another double, and the rout was on. Before the Braves could stop it six runs crossed the plate, and the Giants went on to an 11–2 victory.

In the clubhouse later Rigney remarked to a San Francisco reporter, "Scoring one run in an 11–2 victory doesn't seem like much, but baseball men will tell you that the first run in a game is a psychologically important one. That's what Willie gave us, the one that started things off. And if you'll notice, he's often the guy that bats in or scores the first run for us."

The Braves took the next two games of the series, and it looked again as though they could beat the Giants in the important games, especially since Lew Burdette was due to pitch the final game. Burdette had a lifetime record against the Giants of twenty victories and only seven defeats, and when the Braves rushed into the lead, 5–1, at the end of three innings, it looked like number twenty-one for him. But Willie led off in the fourth inning, starting a rally again with a single. Cepeda followed with a homer, to make the score 5–3. The next inning, with two out and Kirkland on with a walk, Willie singled again, and again Cepeda homered behind him, putting the Giants out in front, 6–5. They went on from there to win, 11–5, making the four-game series a standoff.

Willie's heroics proved extremely costly, however. In the 11–2 victory he had injured his hip colliding with catcher Del Rice as he scored. In the final game of the set he aggravated the injury colliding with catcher Del Crandall. Several days later, his back and hip still sore, he was hit by a thrown ball as he was sliding into second on a steal. The ball smacked him hard on the hip, and Willie cried out in pain. He finished the game, though he could barely hobble through the final innings.

Rigney told him to take a couple of days off. "I'm okay, Skip," Willie protested. "It just hurts like the dickens, that's all."

Rigney persisted. "Playing might cripple you so bad you'd be lost for weeks, and then where would we be? Better that

172

we lose you just for a day or two. When you can walk without a limp, you'll go right back in."

Three days later he was back in the line-up. He went hitless the first day back, got one single off the end of his bat the next. Something was wrong; Willie's hot bat had suddenly grown cold. What was wrong? Could it have been the brief layoff that knocked him off stride? Was the hip injury affecting his swing?

Rigney hesitated to ask, and Willie couldn't say.

The slump continued. Three days, four days, a week. His hits were few, and all singles. Either he went down swinging or the ball dribbled off the end of his bat for an easy infield out. The Giants slipped downward with him. Seeing Willie fail, the confidence of the young players began to falter. The Giants slipped to third place.

Rigney stewed in quiet desperation. He watched Willie carefully, thought he saw what was wrong with his hitting, but he couldn't go to him. There was something holding him back; he wasn't sure himself exactly what it was. But it was that indefinable gap between them, a line he couldn't cross, a line drawn perhaps by the ghost of Leo Durocher that hung over the Giants. For Rigney knew how it had been between Leo and Willie, knew that he had never won the place in Willie's heart that Leo had won—a place perhaps neither he nor any other manager ever could win.

Because he knew that, it might have been pride that held him back. He longed to tell Willie what he had seen as he watched him bat; in addition to all else, he worried that Willie would resent his advice. He was the manager of the Giants, but with Willie it was different. He couldn't be confident that he was that much Willie's manager.

Rigney was sitting in his office, brooding. The Giants were in the locker room outside, dressing quietly. Too quietly, Rigney thought. They were closing out their home stand against the Phillies that afternoon, then would head for Los

Angeles to play the Dodgers. The future was not bright. From .346 Willie had slid to .307, and the whole team was slumping around him. During the two-week home stand the stadium had echoed with jeers for Willie. Rigney sighed, took off his cap, ran a hand over his white hair. Lucky I have hair at all, he thought. He wondered how it would be to quit baseball managing and go into something sane, like stunt flying or tiger hunting. Finally he took a pencil from his desk drawer and began scribbling the day's line-up on a big yellow pad.

In the middle of his writing Willie walked in and sat down. He didn't say a word, just walked in, sat down, and remained there, squeezing his cap between his hands. Rigney finished the line-up and looked at him. "What's up, Willie?" he asked quietly, but in his chest his heart pounded like a thousand drums.

Willie licked his lips, gulped, squeezed his cap some more. "I need your help, Skip." The words came in a rush, a regurgitation, as though they had been pressing on his insides and he couldn't wait to get rid of them. Now, having done so, he seemed to breathe easier, to relax. He looked at his manager cautiously, watching for a reaction, but Rigney was too shaken to speak. His silence emboldened Willie.

"I need help with my hitting," he said. "You the skipper, you see things I can't see. Maybe you know what's wrong. Nobody else is gonna tell me anything."

He's come to me at last, Rigney thought. It's going to be a good year, no matter what else happens. Maybe now that gap would close, that line would disappear. It didn't matter that it might never be the way it was between Willie and Leo. The important thing was that Willie had come to him for help with his problem, and they could work together on it.

"Yes," he said after a moment, "I think I can help, Willie. I've been watching you, and maybe I've spotted what you're

174

doing wrong." He then explained in detail what he had observed during Willie's slump, and added, "But I want you to see it for yourself. Before we do anything I want you to watch out for these things in today's game. Tell me if you think I'm right. If I am, tomorrow we'll go to work on it, early in the morning."

Willie watched. He went hitless again, but it wasn't so depressing this time, because he noticed that what Rigney had told him seemed right, and he knew that he would be able to correct his mistakes with his manager's help. Buoyed by the realization, he sparkled in the field, saving Johnny Antonelli's 3–0 shutout with two sensational catches. Once, with two men on base, he crashed into the right center field fence to rob Harry Anderson of a hit. Three innings later he charged in to make a roll-over shoestring catch of a low line drive by Sparky Anderson. In the shower later, he was positively chipper.

In the Los Angeles Coliseum the next morning, long before the rest of the team reported on field, Willie was there with Rigney, Bill Posedel, the pitching coach, and the batting practice catcher. Posedel took a bag of baseballs and went to the mound. Willie crouched in the batter's box.

"There, see what I mean, Willie?" Rigney said. "You're too far back in the box. Stay there. Bill," he called to the pitching coach, "throw him an outside curve, but over the plate." Posedel, a former pitcher, tried a couple of pitches, then threw one where Rigney wanted it. Willie swung and missed. Posedel threw several more in the same area—over the outside corner of the plate. Willie either missed them or trickled them off the end of his bat.

"Looks like you were right," he said to Rigney.

Rigney nodded. "See what's happening, Willie? Somehow you began standing so deep in the box that the pitchers were able to curve you to death outside. If you hit the ball at all, it was off the end of the bat."

"Well, then all I gotta do," Willie said, "is move in closer, right?"

"Right. But not so fast. While we're moving you, let's try to find just the right spot for you to stand in, and then you keep it. Let's experiment a little."

They worked together like that for almost an hour, Posedel pitching and Willie hitting until their uniforms were stained with sweat and their arms ached. Every once in a while Rigney would shift Willie around, draw diagrams in the batter's box, take the bat himself and imitate Willie's posture at the plate.

After a time Willie began connecting. The ball began to jump from his bat, rattle against the fences, sail into the stands.

"That's it, that's it!" Rigney called encouragement. "Now you're getting your full power into the ball."

Willie stopped for a moment. "But it feels kind of funny, standing up this close," he said.

"So let it feel funny," Rigney said. "You'll get used to it. I don't care if you don't get a hit your next ten times up. If you meet the ball squarely like you're doing now, you'll snap out of it. Now come on, another five minutes and we can call it quits."

Willie hit a few more into the seats, until finally Rigney was satisfied. Then they all went back into the clubhouse to shower and rest and get ready for the game against the Dodgers. After his shower Rigney retired to his office. He was dozing there, waiting for the rest of the team to arrive, when Willie walked in. "I almost forgot." He extended his hand. "Thanks," he said. Rigney looked at his face a moment, smiled and shook Willie's hand.

17

THE LOS ANGELES COLISEUM ROCKED TO THE NOISE OF THE huge crowd. In the brief period of a year the Dodger-Giant rivalry had been transplanted with all its stadium-filling excitement and color. Especially was this so in 1959, when both teams were battling furiously along with the Braves for possession of first place in the National League. Fortunately for the Giants their two-week slump was paralleled by a similar one by the other two contenders, so little ground was lost. As matters stood before the two-game set with Los Angeles, the Braves were first, leading the Dodgers by one game and the Giants by two.

The importance of this brief meeting between the two clubs was evident, therefore. The Braves were idle for two days except for an exhibition benefit game. By winning both games, the Dodgers could pull into a tie for the league lead; the Giants, by winning two, could climb over the Dodgers and trail by only one.

Rigney started Jack Sanford against the Dodgers' Roger Craig, and moved Willie up to second in the batting order, replacing him in the third spot with Kirkland. Davenport, leading off the game, hit a home run, and the Giants were ahead quickly. The Dodgers struck back with two in their half of the first, then the Giants led again, scoring two in the third on a solid single by Willie and a home run by Kirkland. When Willie trotted into the dugout after scoring he sat down next to Rigney. "Still not getting good wood on it," he complained. "I told you, I feel a little funny standing so close to the plate."

Rigney reassured him. "Have a little patience, Willie. You got to admit you're looking better already. Even that fly ball you hit in the first inning was better than anything you hit in a week." Willie nodded. "You the boss, Skip."

The Dodgers tied the score again in their half of the third, 3–3, then Sanford and Craig tightened up. Neither team could score again through the eighth. In the ninth the Giants broke the tie on a triple by Brandt after Cepeda had singled. And again the Dodgers tied the score, sending the game into extra innings. Through the tenth, the eleventh, the twelfth the teams struggled.

The Giants began the thirteenth with the top of the batting order. Davenport brought groans to the Dodger fans by hitting Craig for his second homer of the day, putting the Giants ahead 4–3. But one run was not enough to insure the win. Then Willie stepped in to hit. He bent over and rubbed dirt on his hands. In the tenth inning he had really banged one, but Furillo had caught up with it in right center field. He stepped into the batter's box carefully, mentally drawing the squares he and Rigney had boxed out that morning. Then he dug in and waited for Craig's pitch. It was a good one, a fast ball over the outside corner. Willie swung. The ball leaped from his bat, sailed high and deep to left field, up and well over the screen for a home run. He was grinning from ear to ear as he rounded the bases, and the sullen silence of the Dodger rooters was music to him. He plopped into the dugout, accepted handshakes all around, then winked and said to Rigney, "Some bunt, eh, Skip?"

178

Rigney gulped hard. He hadn't heard a quip like that from Willie in two years.

The Giants won the game, 6–4, which put them in a tie for second with the Dodgers. But for the victory to have significance, they had to follow it up with another one over the Dodgers or find themselves no better off than they were two days ago.

This time Sam Jones faced Don Drysdale. Pitching magnificently, Jones threw a one-hitter, giving up only a scratch single to Jim Gilliam. And Willie provided the margin for his 2–0 victory by hitting a home run in the third inning with Davenport on base.

Now the Giants were in second place. What was more important, Willie was definitely out of his long slump. And as he broke out, so did the rest of the Giants. Kirkland, Spencer, Cepeda woke up. There was chatter on the bench, on the field, in the clubhouse. The team came alive again. Rigney began to think that maybe everything would turn out all right after all.

The pennant race continued its frantic pace, the three contenders battling fiercely all the way. Extra inning games were frequent; ninth inning rallies were expected, rather than merely hoped for. Tenaciously the Braves kept their lead. Just as tenaciously the Giants and Dodgers dogged their heels. A week after the Dodger-Giant meeting, the Dodgers met the Braves in Milwaukee while the Giants were in Cincinnati. The league order put the Braves ahead by half a game over the Giants, and a full game over the Dodgers.

Willie had continued to hit, getting at least one safety in every game since the first one after his practice session with Rigney. The Cincinnati trip had been preceded by the All-Star game and Willie, playing in his sixth straight All-

Star contest, was the hero of the 5–4 victory, driving in the winning run with a triple in the eighth inning.

Now in Cincinnati a golden opportunity awaited. While the Dodgers and the Braves were grappling, the Giants could take advantage of the second division Reds and move into the league lead. The Reds were not eager to co-operate, however. That same day Freddie Hutchinson had taken over as the Cincinnati manager, succeeding Mayo Smith, and he was anxious to make his debut a winning one. He started Don Newcombe, the perennial Giant nemesis, against Sam Jones.

For five innings the game was scoreless, while the scoreboard showed that in Milwaukee the Dodgers and Braves were tied, 3–3. In the sixth the Giants scored twice, but single runs in the seventh and eighth tied the score for the Reds. As Willie stepped up to hit in the top of the ninth, he looked at the scoreboard. The Dodgers had won, 4–3, dropping the Braves into a tie with the Giants. This was the opportunity of the season, the first chance to take over the league lead.

Willie let Newcombe's first pitch go by for a strike. The next one was a curve over the outside that Willie stroked for a single to left field. Cepeda flied out next, and Spencer came up to hit. Willie thought out the situation. When Cepeda was at the plate, he had been content to wait at first, since Orlando was a long ball hitter. But Spencer did not have Cepeda's power, was a singles and doubles hitter. That meant that a hit by Spencer could not score him unless he was on second.

Willie watched Newcombe carefully. And Newcombe watched Willie just as carefully. On the second pitch to Spencer, Willie was off, and easily beat the throw from catcher Henry Dotterer. On the next pitch Spencer tapped a grounder to shortstop. Eddie Kasko came in fast, but threw to first too late. Willie kept on running, rounded third, sped for home. First baseman Frank Robinson threw to the plate, but Willie was in safely with a headfirst slide.

180

Jones set the Reds down in the last half of the ninth and the Giants won, 4–3, putting them in first place, half a game ahead of the Braves and the Dodgers.

From the celebrating in the Giant clubhouse afterward, a visitor might have assumed the pennant had just been won. There were grins all around, with horseplay and much singing in the showers. Rigney tried to hold them down, but his grin exposed his own exuberance. "Take it easy, take it easy," he walked around saying. "It's only July. We got a long way to go."

But there was a confidence among the Giants that bordered dangerously on euphoria. What could go wrong? was the feeling. The pitchers are going great, the hitters are hitting and Willie Mays is winning ball games again. In truth, as the days and the weeks flew by, the Giants' confidence seemed warranted. With Willie hitting like the Mays of old, they widened their lead to a full game, to two games, to three games as Willie pulled out a ninth inning victory with a two-run homer.

The pennant race swung into August with the Giants still in front, faltering here and there along the way, but bouncing back in time to keep their lead. On August 7th, playing at home against Cincinnati, they were in front by one game. They beat Cincinnati that day, but sliding back to first base after a single, Willie jammed the little finger of his right hand against the bag. He called for a time out. The finger began to swell rapidly. Running over from his coaching box at third, Rigney looked at it, called for a pinch runner for Willie and sent him into the clubhouse to have it checked by the trainer.

Rigney had to keep him out of the line-up for the next two games, though he called on him to pinch hit in each case. Willie grounded out both times. The next day he insisted that Rigney return him to the line-up.

"How about the finger?" Rigney wanted to know.

"It's okay," Willie said.

Rigney looked at it. "Still looks swollen to me. Maybe we ought to X-ray it. Could be you broke a bone."

"Don't need no X-ray," Willie said. "It feels sore a little, that's all. I can play."

Rigney thought a moment. "Okay, if you say so, Willie. I'll announce to the reporters that you'll play today."

"Don't say nothing about the finger, Rig," Willie said. "I don't want anybody to think I'm looking for an alibi or anything."

"They're gonna ask, anyway."

"Tell them it's nothing. It's okay."

Rigney looked at him searchingly. He understood. "Okay, if that's how you want it, Willie. We'll keep it quiet about the finger."

It was a trial to keep the promise, for Willie's hitting fell off badly after that. Every time he hit the ball off the end of his bat it stung so that his eyes rolled with the pain. He played every day with the finger bent and swollen at the second joint, stiffened with hot agony along its entire length. But he refused to ask for a rest, refused to explain the cause of his poor hitting, though the boos from the fans cascaded upon him with ever-increasing intensity and the sports writers began to mumble about an "Eighty-thousand-dollar pop-out."

Fortunately for the Giants at that moment they received batting help in the form of Willie McCovey, the first baseman from Phoenix whom Willie had pointed out in spring training. McCovey came up in August and broke in sensationally, giving the Giants a lift at the plate in the nick of time.

Now the San Francisco fans had another hero to cheer, while jeering Willie Mays. Only Rigney and trainer Bowman knew the truth, knew the agony in which Willie played, knew that even hitting now below .300 he meant more to the team

182

in so many ways than the new slugger from the minor leagues. The deception undoubtedly would have gone on for the remainder of the season had not a New York sports writer visited San Francisco to cover the climax of the pennant fight.

Milton Gross of the New York *Post* walked into the Giants' locker room at Seals Stadium and greeted Willie warmly. Then he shook hands, and started at the audible gasp that escaped Willie. "What's up, what did I do?" he asked, alarmed. Willie held up the injured finger. "It's broken or fractured," he said. "Don't say nothing about it."

"That's why you haven't been hitting," Gross said.

"I can't swing right," Willie admitted. "I've been throwing myself at the ball, but I don't want anybody knowing about it. I don't want anybody to think I'm setting up an alibi."

"What did the doctor say?" Gross wanted to know.

"Haven't seen one. They want me to, but I want to stay in and play. I can help the club in the field, if I can't at the plate. I know Mr. Stoneham would want me to play at a time like this and that man's been as good to me as any man I've ever known. I don't care if I hit two hundred as long as I can do something to help us win. The team needs me in the field now more than at the plate, anyway, the way McCovey's been hitting."

Gross left Willie and sought out Rigney, confronting him with Willie's story. Rigney sighed. "Willie doesn't think I know how much it hurts, but I do. I promised though that I'd keep quiet. The last thing he would want is to have anybody think he's looking for an excuse."

Gross nodded. "But I made no such promise and I'm going to print the story. Willie deserves to have it known why he's hitting only two ninety-six, that he's been playing for a month with a broken finger."

"Good," Rigney said. "But you understand he's still going

183

to play. He wants to, and I need him. Willie with a broken finger is better than any three men I could put out there in his place. We're holding onto the lead by the skin of our teeth—and Willie's broken finger. I take Willie out now, with only two weeks left to play, and I can kiss the pennant good-by."

Gross printed the story next day, despite Willie's protests and embarrassment. The boos for Willie quieted, and there was even occasional applause as some of the fans showed their appreciation for his spartan behavior. He ignored the applause as he had ignored the jeers. His mind was intent on one thing—the pennant.

On September 17th the Giants played their last game at home. After that they would wind up the last eight games of the season on the road. The tension was electric in Seals Stadium. The Giants led the league by one slim game, and this final contest at home was against the Braves, panting on their heels in second place.

Before the game, columnist Gross approached Willie. "How do you feel?" he asked.

Willie laughed grimly. "Sore all over. But I go nine."

Warren Spahn, the Braves pitcher, didn't survive the first inning. Eddie Bressoud opened with a single, McCovey walked, Willie singled and Cepeda singled for two runs, chasing Spahn, bringing in relief pitcher Carleton Willey.

In the second inning, after Bressoud homered, Willie singled for his second straight hit. In the fourth he homered with two men on base to give the Giants an 8–0 lead. In the seventh inning he drove in another run with a single, his fourth straight hit, as the Giants walloped Milwaukee, 13–6, extending their lead to two games.

There was dancing in the dressing room after that victory. All San Francisco was preparing to celebrate its first pennant. The Giants were two games ahead with just eight games to go, and with a broken finger Willie was going four for four. Who could beat a team like that?

In the Giants' clubhouse Rigney rushed right over to Willie. "You're really something," he exclaimed, embracing him.

Willie tried to steer the conversation elsewhere. "How about that Sam Jones, the way he came in there in relief, wasn't he great? And Davenport at third, he's gonna be some ballplayer."

"How about you, Willie?" a local reporter asked. "Is this your greatest day?"

"Did I go over three hundred?" Willie asked.

The reporter checked his notes. "Yep. You're hitting three hundred and three now. And those five runs batted in gave you an even hundred."

Willie nodded. "Good."

"You're playing ball now the way Willie Mays plays," a San Francisco writer said to him.

Willie bristled. His body ached. His finger throbbed and burned. "Listen, I don't think that's fair," he said. "I only know one way to play. It's easy to say I'm playing like Willie Mays when I get four hits."

"What I mean is," the reporter explained, "you're running into walls, making great catches and all."

"I been doing it for eight years," Willie said wearily. "It didn't start today."

The San Francisco sports writers, who had in recent weeks begun to recognize Willie as the great ballplayer everyone else had acknowledged him to be, turned to Rigney. "Think this one will do it?" they asked him.

Rigney grinned. "Could be. Could be this one was the pennant."

Nobody could explain what happened next. The Giants moved into Los Angeles and lost three straight to the

185

Dodgers, falling right through to third place as the Braves also won three straight.

Then they lost two out of three to Chicago and, on the final day of the season, with their only hope a tie if they won their double-header and both the Dodgers and Braves lost, they lost twice to the Cardinals.

The sudden collapse was so mystifying that they staggered home to San Francisco in a daze. Everything seemed to go to pieces at once. The hitters failed in the clutch and the pitchers couldn't get a man out. Of the hitters only the two Willies—Mays and McCovey—kept going until the final out in St. Louis. Of the pitchers only Jones won in that final terrible week.

Nobody could explain it. But with the 1959 pennant within an inch of their grasp, the Giants let it get away, finishing third. When they landed at the airport that final evening, the brass bands and cheering crowds that had been planned the week before were now only porters and the wives of the players, greeting them in sympathetic silence. The following afternoon Rigney held a brief meeting in the clubhouse while the players packed their bags. What could he tell them but that they all had done a great job, better than anyone had expected, and, in effect, wait till next year?

He sought out Willie when the meeting broke up and the men began to file from the clubhouse. "Better give that finger a thorough examination," he said. "The club's got a good doctor here in town."

Willie shook his head. "I'll have it checked in New York. I'm going right back there with Marghurite. We're selling our house here, moving back to New York."

Rigney looked at him questioningly.

"Oh, I'm not mad at anybody, Skip," Willie said, understanding the look. "But I got started there and most of my friends are there. New York is my town, that's all."

Rigney nodded. "Best of luck from me, whatever you do.

You know with me, Willie, you'll always be the greatest."

The manager of the Giants was hardly alone in his estimation of Willie. Horace Stoneham, president of the club, wasted no time announcing that Willie would get a salary raise to $85,000 for 1960.

Then, when the 1959 World Series had been wrapped up in the Dodgers' favor and the awards for the season were being handed out, they invented a new one for Willie, who had won just about all there were in the books.

A special committee of the Baseball Writers of America named him "The Most Exciting Player in Baseball."

"We can't hope ever to see another player like him," part of the award read. "A man like Willie Mays comes along just once in a lifetime."

WILLIE MAYS

Born: Fairfield, Alabama
May 6, 1931

Bats right
Throws right

Height: 5' 10½"
Weight: 175 pounds

Year	Club	League	Pos	G	AB	R	H	2B	3B	HR	RBI	SB	Avg
1950	Trenton	Inter-St.	OF	81	306	50	108	20	8	4	55	7	.353
1951	Minneapolis	A.A.	OF	35	149	38	71	18	3	8	30	5	.477
1951	New York	N.L.	OF	121	464	59	127	22	5	20	68	7	.274
1952	New York	N.L.	OF	34	127	17	30	2	4	4	23	4	.236
1952-53	New York	N.L.		(In U.S. Army)									
1954	New York	N.L.	OF	151	565	119	195	33	13*	41	110	8	.345*
1955	New York	N.L.	OF	152	580	123	185	18	13*	51*	127	24	.319
1956	New York	N.L.	OF	152	578	101	171	27	8	36	84	40*	.296
1957	New York	N.L.	OF	152	585	112	195	26	20*	35	97	38*	.333
1958	San Francisco	N.L.	OF	152	600	121*	208	33	11	29	96	31*	.347
1959	San Francisco	N.L.	OF	151	575	125	180	43	5	34	104	27*	.313
Major League Totals			8 yrs.	1065	4074	777	1291	204	79	250	709	179	.317

* Indicates led league.

World Series Record

Year	Club	League	Pos	G	AB	R	H	2B	3B	HR	RBI	SB	Avg
1951	New York	N.L.	OF	6	22	1	4	0	0	0	1	0	.182
1954	New York	N.L.	OF	4	14	4	4	1	0	0	3	1	.286
World Series Totals				10	36	5	8	1	0	0	4	1	.222

Chart by Seymour Siwoff, Elias Baseball Bureau, New York City

Index

Mays, Willie, childhood and youth, 11-28; plays semi-pro ball, 22; with Birmingham Barons, 26-34; his first professional game, 26-27; helps family financially, 29; is scouted by major leagues, 31; his 1949 season, 31; on barnstorming tour, 31-34; is streak hitter, 32; is signed by Giants, 37; with Trenton, 38-41; acquires nickname, 40-41; is promoted to Millers, 41-45; his meeting with Durocher, 41; Giants' scout's report on him, 42-43; is called up to Giants, 45; at 20, 46; wears No. 24, 47; fails to hit, 50-53; feels self-doubt, 56; is encouraged by Durocher, 57-58; is dropped to eighth spot, 58; makes sensational catch, 58-59; is told to ignore slurs, 61-62; continues to spark club, 64; makes spectacular throw, 66; steals off Spahn, 67-68; in play-off against Dodgers, 69-71; against Yankees in World Series, 72-75; is named Rookie of the Year, 75; returns home for visit, 77-79; in Army, 83; death of his mother, 83; hurts ankle, 83; rejoins Giants, 84; is still streak hitter, 88; Durocher helps him, 89-90; wins crucial game, 92; is on All-Star team, 92-93; death of his Aunt Sarah, 93; is idol of fans, 94; is assigned personal adviser, 95; moves to Mrs. Goosby's, 99; changes batting stance, 101-03; Willie Mays Day, 103; inspires teammates, 103-04; plays stickball with boys, 105-06; wins batting championship, 107; his 1954 record, 107; against Indians in World Series, 108-10; is honored, 110; plays winter baseball, 111; is given raise, 112; weariness affects playing, 114; is booed, 115; is benched, 116; returns to form, 118; his 1955 record, 119; is distressed at Durocher's resignation, 119; marriage of, 121; hopes he and Rigney get along, 123; is still compared to greatest players, 123; on stolen base rampage, 124, 126; goes into slump, 126; is fined, 129; his 1956 record, 130; interview with sports writers, 132-34; makes fourth All-Star team, 137; farewell to Polo Grounds, 137-38; his 1957 record, 138; has trouble buying home, 140-41; is highest paid Giant, 142; helps rookies, 145-46; in slump again, 146-49, 153; is hospitalized, 149-51; returns to line-up, 152; his 1958 record, 156; adopts baby boy, 156; is compared with Mantle, 157-59; is not too popular in San Francisco, 159-62; at 28, 162; hurts leg, 163-65; is booed, 169, 182; is injured again, 172; is helped by Rigney, 175-76; plays with broken finger, 181-85; is moving back to New York City, 186; is given special award, 187

Meyer, Jack, 119
Miller, Stu, 132, 146, 163, 169
Millers, Minneapolis, 41-45, 143
Milwaukee, Wisconsin, 42, 93, 116, 154, 171, 179-80
Minneapolis, Minnesota, 44, 47, 117
Mize, Johnny, 119
Mizell, Vinegar Bend, 126
Modica, Pete, 86
Monarchs, Kansas City, 26, 28, 29, 30
Montague, Ed, 35-37
Monzant, Ramon, 146, 152, 163
Moore, Terry, 53
Morgan, Bobby, 80
Mossi, Don, 114
"Most Exciting Player in Baseball, The," 187
Most Valuable Player awards, 72, 110
Mueller, Don, 43, 70, 72, 88, 91, 103, 106-07, 127, 132
Murray, Arch, 82, 122
Musial, Stan, 53, 60, 91, 137, 138, 148, 158

Narleski, Ray, 114
National League, 54, 60, 69, 73, 81, 93, 110, 137, 138, 152, 177
Neeman, Cal, 137
Negro League, 13, 24-34
New Jersey, 104, 120
New York City, 29, 36, 42, 43, 45, 67, 69, 81, 94, 97, 118, 121, 134, 139, 149, 186
Newcombe, Don, 23, 30, 32, 34, 62, 69-70, 106, 169, 180
Noble, Ray, 59, 72

O'Connell, Danny, 131-32, 136, 155
Orioles, Baltimore, 123, 163
Orlando, Florida, 41
Ott, Mel, 52, 94, 106, 138, 158-59

Perry, Lou, 34-36
Pafko, Andy, 71
Paige, Satchel, 32
Philadelphia, Pennsylvania, 45-46, 51, 68, 151
Phillies, Philadelphia, 49-51, 59, 68, 107, 114, 118, 125, 149, 152, 162, 169
Phillips, Taylor, 155
Phoenix, Arizona, 79-80, 84, 113, 122,

About the Author

MILTON J. SHAPIRO was born in Brooklyn, New York, attended P. S. 115 and Boys High School there. At college (C.C.N.Y.) he majored in advertising and public relations and was editor of *Ticker,* the undergraduate newspaper. While a senior, he got a job as copy boy on a New York newspaper and six months later moved up to the Sports Department where he covered all the major sports, particularly baseball. He later became sports editor for The New York *Enquirer.* In his spare time he started writing sports biographies, and has become one of the most popular writers in that field. He and his family now live on Long Island and he commutes to his job in New York City where he is managing editor of a national gun magazine.